HR
@
THE HEART OF BUSINESS

HR @ THE HEART OF BUSINESS

Edited by

T V RAO
A GANGOPADHYAY
R S S MANI

EXCEL BOOKS

ISBN: 81-7446-320-8

First Edition: New Delhi, 2002

EXCEL BOOKS
A-45, Naraina, Phase-I
New Delhi-110028

Published by Anurag Jain for Excel Books, A-45, Naraina, Phase-I, New Delhi -110 028
and printed by him at Excel Printers, C-206, Naraina, Phase-I, New Delhi -110 028

contents

►HR PROCESSES FOR VALUE ADDITION◄

preface

The National HRD Network has always been known for its contemporary approach in choosing relevant conference themes. To go down memory lane,The National HRD Network was formed with participants sharing their Recent Experiences in HRD in 1985. The first conference in 1987 focused on the "Alternatives Strategies and Approached to HRD" where several CEOs have shared their success experiences. When an issue was raised on whether HRD is getting limited to Managers, the next conference focused on the HRD for workmen and brought out the publication on Organizational Effectiveness and Excellence in HRD though quality circles and other innovations. The next symposium focused on the Role of HRD Managers and the methods of developing HRD Profession. Subsequent conferences focused on Internationalization, Globalization, Mergers and Acquisitions and such other themes. Every conference devoted to some degree the HRD interventions in the not for profit sector.

The current challenge HRD is facing is to become a business partner. It has been recognized that HRD can be a business driver. It is no more a service function. It is established beyond doubt that people can provide technological, financial, leadership and managerial advantage to corporations. They need to be chosen carefully, developed, nurtured, utilized and their competencies multiplied. How are corporations approaching this important task? What are the experiences available? What is the role HR is playing in driving this change and changing itself as a driver? This is the focal theme of this conference.

The theme deals with the economic challenges faced by the Indian economy, role of HR in the business in the current scenario, HR strategies followed by various corporations in the current scenario, critical HR processes needed for long term development of corporations and the ways and means of enhancing the effectiveness of the HR function

In this volume we are presenting 14 papers carefully selected from among the various papers sent to us for presentation at the conference.

The papers deal with the following themes:

1. Role of HR;
2. HR and OD Interventions for enhancing organizational effectiveness
3. HR processes for value addition.

The common theme running behind these papers is to enhance the impact of HR as business drive. We hope that the readers will find this enjoyable.

- DR T V RAO
- DR A GANGOPADHYAY
- PROF R S S MANI
Editorial Committee

►Role of HR◄

CHAPTER

1

inclusive corporation HR role in attracting and retaining diverse workforce

C S VENKATA RATNAM & G P RAO*

* Dr C S Venkata Ratnam is Professor, International Management Institute, New Delhi and Director, Gitam Institute of Foreign Trade. Mr. G P Rao is Vice President (HR), Birla VXL Ltd., New Delhi and Secretary, National HRD Network.

An inclusive corporation affirms diversity. It consciously and deliberately pursues policies and programmes to create a culture and climate for all people from diverse backgrounds to harness their talent and potential fully. This paper is presented in three parts. Part 1 presents five reasons why organizations need to become heterogeneous and inclusive in their staffing policies. Part 2 highlights, with the example of a case, how to become – or what it takes to become - an inclusive corporation. The third part shows the advantages and sustainability of a strategy to become an inclusive corporation.

FROM EXCLUSION TO INCLUSION

Traditionally, industrial and business organizations in every society had staffing policies that excluded more people than not. For a long time in the USA, it was white males. In India, it was brahmanical. Only 'males for sales' syndrome persisted for long even in the West. The glass ceiling for women meant corporates 'fishing in half the pond' when it came to groping or grooming talent or filling vacancies in the top echelons of the corporate hierarchy. But this is changing for reasons such as the following:

1. Changing demographics of workforce make it imperative for corporates to put in place 'family friendly' policies to let workers with family responsibilities balance the needs of both work and family. The emergence of virtual organizations meant virtual workplaces that remove the distinction between work and home: work is home and home is work.
2. When work is changing from muscle to mind and brawn to brain, there is a shift in staffing patterns. Homogeneous work force continues to be preferred when work is by and large physical. Heterogeneity is encouraged when work is knowledge based.
3. When creativity and innovation hold the key to or form the basis for competitiveness and radical improvement in performance is critical to success, corporates need workforce with diverse backgrounds so that they can think differently, 'outside the box' and 'upside down.'
4. Cultural fit or the lack of it accounts for the difference between success and failure whether it is in start-ups or in mergers and acquisitions. The key

challenge for managers – both HR and line – is to acquire a heterogeneous workforce and blend them into a homogeneous group, engineering a common culture. Managing difference is an important skill that every manager must necessarily possess and sharpen.

5. Globalization has widened social inequities and tensions. It is increasingly becoming imperative that the characteristics of workforce must reflect the characteristics of communities in which they operate and the markets they serve.

At a workshop on the subject organized by National HRD Network in association with two business schools – International Management Institute, New Delhi and Gitam Institute of Foreign Trade, Visakhapatnam - Dr. S. Chandrashekhar, President (HR), Reliance Infocom observed that in the future tolerant corporations will succeed more than intolerant corporations. He identified gender diversity, cross cultural identities, caste and religious identities, operating style differences which bring about a change in diversification as some of the key issues. Building corporate culture should incorporate strategies for managing workforce diversity. This can be done by mapping the social cultural differences, choosing the right people for initial encounters, selecting the cultural intelligence and blending the diverse operating styles.

Corporates need to build a team of tolerant corporate managers who would manage the diversity from cross cultural identities. Benefits from cultural diversity could help in expanding the vision in the corporate world. The key is to build a tolerant corporation where tolerance will be the foundation of a resilient corporation.

How To Be An Inclusive Corporation – A Case Study

This case relates to a particular U.S. multinational in information technology sector with manufacturing and marketing operations in India. It supplies computer hardware and peripherals. Among the fundamental principles and rights at work (FPRW) under discussion, the case highlights the commitment of a multinational to the principle of non-discrimination and equality of opportunity. The case study recognizes that multinational and transnational companies are transmission belts for the dissemination of best practises in human resource management. It also shows how the host country (U.S.A.) philosophy and practises are internalized in the guest country (India).

ENTERPRISE PROFILE. ABC Limited (real name disguised pending clearance from the company) is the Indian subsidiary of U.S. based transnational company. It produces and sells computer hardware and peripherals. Its brand equity in the market puts it among the top five players in the market. It is well regarded globally for its very proactive policies in building and managing a diverse workforce. The company considers diverse workforce as an imperative business need in terms of tapping from a wider pool of talent as well as to encourage creativity and innovation that a heterogeneous workforce provides. Being a global company, it wants the demographic composition of its workforce to broadly reflect the demographic composition of its customer base. Towards the dawn of the new millennium, a woman became the CEO at its headquarters.

The company employs 1500 persons. The company monitors the workforce composition in terms of gender. It has achieved gender parity at the lower levels (upto manager) and is striving to achieve gender parity at senior levels too in the next five years. It is consciously trying to ensure that the regional representation of workforce is consistent with the sales revenue from the respective regions, but is finding it difficult due to uneven supply of and response to company's recruitment from among people with relevant skills. As such there is a relatively heavier representation from south and north as opposed to west and east. The company was rather reluctant to share exact numbers of people in different categories and their demographic background. The company does not measure composition of workforce in terms of caste which is one of the most sensitive aspects in India, but not critical in the U.S.

Over the past 10 years, it has It is non-unionized, not only in India but also in all other countries where it operates. The company says it is not averse to unions and it does not have any anti-union policy. There was no effort at unionization, any time in the past.

KEY ISSUES IN MANAGEMENT PHILOSOPHY. The key issue for the company is to get the right people in the right place at the right time to meet the company's business objectives. Hiring the best-qualified people is fundamental to company's success. Highly capable, innovative, and flexible people are the foundation of the company's competitive position. The company must select, attract, and retain people with skills and attributes in line with the company's long-term needs.

The company consciously endeavours to become an equal opportunity employer. Its commitment to affirmative action is such that it tells its managers that it should be demonstrated during every phase of the staff process, viz., recruitment, selection, placement, training and development, transfer, reward and promotion. The human resource department is responsible for coordinating the staffing function. This department will offer assistance and counsel as needed, although final decisions rest with the hiring manager. Individual managers are responsible for and made accountable to realizing the company's affirmative action policies and programmes with appropriate inputs in their performance planning and review process.

PERCEPTION OF THE PROBLEM. The company believes that traditionally companies in the U.S. recruited white males and companies in India recruited males from the elite sections of the society, i.e., so-called forward communities for its professional and managerial jobs. By ignoring women and not allowing them opportunities to grow, they realized that in both the countries they were 'fishing in half the pond'. Company's diversity programmes not only aimed at ending such discrimination and corrected the social evil, but also made great business sense in letting them pick up talent from a wider pool.

The company found that while discrimination in the U.S. was mainly based on gender and colour, in India it is mainly based on gender and caste. There are differences in the approaches of both the countries in dealing with the problem of discrimination. The U.S. focuses on goals and timetables (Equal Employment Opportunities guidelines) while India believed in reservation in education and employment (through constitutional provisions and supportive legislative and administrative provisions) for its disadvantaged groups, including women and minorities. In the U.S., the non-discrimination guidelines apply to both the private and the public sectors while in India they are mainly applied in government and the public sector. In this context, the initiative of multinational corporations in promoting diversity and equal employment opportunity in their Indian operations merit special mention and appreciation. It must be added, though, that the multinational corporations in India target gender equality but do not usually have any measures to fight caste discrimination.

A senior executive observed that the company does not want to discriminate people on caste lines, but could not establish goals and timetables to recruit socially disadvantaged communities. The company says that in the U.S. the goals and timetables are based on the proportion of candidates from target groups with relevant qualifications and experience for positions at different levels. India introduced reservation policy without looking at the supply side and therefore there are problems in addressing the issue fully. One of the ways to make progress in this direction, an executive of the company said, was to introduce scholarships for persons from target groups in select educational institutions and 'other things being equal' offer them employment opportunities.

ESSENCE AND FORM OF THE 'GOOD POLICIES'. Being a transnational company of the 21st century, the company must in itself be reflective of the varied customer base it seeks to serve.

- Customers, suppliers and strategic partners are increasingly global and multicultural: ABC Limited must be positioned to relate to them.
- Customers are changing – their needs and expectations for products and services are diverse. ABC Limited must be able to understand, connect and respond.
- ABC's competitive advantage is to become the leader in innovation, creativity, problem-solving and organizational flexibility. ABC Limited must have diverse perspectives and talents to meet his global challenge.
- The workforce demographics are changing in most countries. The labour pool is shrinking and labour shortages are projected.

To ensure success, the company must be the best place to work for everyone.

COMPANY POLICIES AND SHARED PRACTISES. ABC Limited has continued to grow and change as a company, ensuring that their policies and practises support their core beliefs and values, their guiding principles and their goals, to make themselves the best place to work for every employee.

These are some of the policies and practises that support ABC diversity and work/ life success.

a) Policies

- Electronic job posting
- Harassment-free work environment
- Domestic partner benefits
- Non-discrimination policy
- Employee network group guidelines
- Open door policy
- Education assistance programme
- Employee assistance programme

b) Shared Practises

- Open communication
- Management by objectives
- Share in company's success
- Provide development opportunities
- Value diversity
- Pay among leaders
- Flexible work hours
- Safe and pleasant work environment

DIVERSITY IN ACTION. Initiatives that help to move from awareness to action include:

a) Development Programmes

At ABC Limited, development programmes increase development opportunities to retain top talent viz:

- (Global) Accelerated development programme (ADP) is a yearlong accelerated management development programme for high potential mid-level managers. Its objective is to advance leadership skills and knowledge, and to establish mentoring relationships. Its goal is to identify, develop and increase the number of diverse candidates for senior management positions.

- (US) Leadership effectiveness and development programme (LEAD) is a formalized leadership development opportunity for high potential/high performing employees. It is designed to develop leadership skills, knowledge and mentoring relationships to enhance career development options and opportunities.

b) Employee Participation

ABC Limited encourages dialogue and open communications. It involves and empowers its workforce:

- Employee network groups that foster employee communication, professional development and teamwork are supported throughout the world.
- Diversity advisory boards, councils and task forces are encouraged in every organization to establish priorities and actions to support local initiatives.

c) Management Leadership

The company's managers strive to achieve the company's diversity and work/life objectives through:

- Diversity action council develops and drives key diversity and work/life initiatives worldwide. It is composed of senior executives representing the company's businesses and related corporate functions.
- Diversity Accountability Framework describes the fundamental behaviours/actions needed from every manager in order to accomplish diversity objectives and the measure that will reflect success.

d) Outreach and Recruitment

At ABC Limited, the aim is to expand candidate pools and increase access to opportunities:

- Targeted college recruiting programmes, including SEED (Student Employment and Development Programme) to facilitate early identification of top candidates and strengthen relationships with diverse candidates and organizations.
- External search firms are identified, and relationships are established to assist in increasing diverse hiring resources.
- Diversity-focused advertisement campaigns are being developed to enhance ability to communicate and attract diverse candidates to the company.
- Expanding access to higher-level job openings is increasing opportunities.
- Education programme is a programme that invests in the future workforce. Its goals are: (a) to ensure early learning readiness, (b) to improve proficiency in science and math, (c) to increase the number of women and minorities in science/math disciplines for future candidate pools.

e) Diversity Resources

At ABC Limited, diversity resources create awareness and inspire action:

- Diversity education and training strategy establishes a consistent delivery of diversity education. It describes the array of educational options that are available to the company worldwide to meet its diversity training needs.
- Diversity best practises forums provide opportunities for ABC Limited to learn from others. Best practises' sharing has been a highlighted feature of the company's management and diversity specialist forums, and other communications.
- Diversity internal web site supports ABC worldwide. It includes online tools, such as diversity presentation materials, diversity education resources and other diversity resource information.

Managing Work-life Demands. ABC Limited provides a broad range of programmes and activities to help employees manage commitments in their work and personal life. A variety of tools and services help employees save time, energy and reduce stress.

- ***Flexible Work Arrangements.*** More than 15% of ABC's employees use alternatives to traditional Monday through Friday work arrangements. These include part-time, telecommuting, job shares and variable work schedules.
- ***Flexibility Practises.*** ABC is one of the first companies in the world to experiment with flexible work hours. Employees can arrive at work any time within a specified window at the beginning of the shift. Its Flexible Time Off (FTO) programme allows the employee to use paid time off in daily half-day or even hourly increments. FTO may be used for rest and recreation, vacation, personal business, personal illness or illness of family members.
- ***Reinventing Work.*** This programme helps work teams examine work processes with a work/life focus. It provides a framework for managers and employees to address job demands and work pressure issues.
- ***Dependent Care Resource and Referral.*** ABC Limited provides a variety of resources and referral services for employees who have dependent care responsibilities for children, elders, people with disabilities, etc.
- ***Working Parent Network.*** ABC Limited supports a variety of working parent networks in which employees share resources, tools and other services.

The company's motives are clear. Diversity and equal opportunity is the goal. It understands that workforce composition should reflect the composition of the community if the business is local (like in a retail store) and customer base if the business is global (as in ABC Limited). It has a vision which is shared worldwide by employees at all levels through education and training and reinforced through performance review and reward systems. The purpose is not just to give women and minorities a chance, but to create an inclusive environment 'where everyone will do their best.' The company has a deliberate strategy to create a heterogeneous culture so that employees from diverse backgrounds contribute not just to productivity, but add value through creativity and innovation. Many of these policies either derive inspiration from or uphold the ILO Convention and Recommendation on 'Workers' With Family Responsibilities.'

BENEFITS AND HOW TO SUSTAIN THE STRATEGY TO BECOME AND REMAIN AN INCLUSIVE CORPORATION?

As a result of the many initiatives to manage diversity in human resources, the company has benefited in the form of having a nurtured, versatile and highly skilled workforce that in many ways stands at the vanguard of superior performance.

The programmes helped ABC Limited to retain talent. Its attrition rates have been 5 per cent lower than the industry average during the past 10 years. At Rs 1,00,000 cost per recruitment, it helped the company save a couple of million rupees every year. The company has been able to advance leadership skills and knowledge, and establish mentoring relationships further leading to an increase in diverse candidates for senior management positions.

The company has also been able to promote personal responsibility and accountability for employee career development for women and other disadvantaged groups.

Employee participation programmes have led to enhanced employee communication, professional development and teamwork. Local initiatives to aid the above have always received encouragement from the central higher authorities in the company.

The company's managers have achieved the company's work/life objectives because of the efforts of the diversity action councils that operate worldwide and diversity accountability framework that describes actions required from employees to fulfill company's HR objectives.

Efforts have also been successfully made to increase employees' pool of skills and thereby opportunities open to them through extensive education programmes.

Active cross-functional employee learning is facilitated with the help of the diversity best practices forum.

The company says that it believes in going beyond legal compliance. Legal compliance has its costs. But non-compliance too has its costs. It is better to be proactive and go beyond legal minimalism. It is difficult to quantify gains as a result of each of the programmes and policies. It is addressing the root causes of discrimination rather than dealing with symptoms. It is grafting the roots to change the leaves and crafting a culture to move in a desired direction where people look at it not just in terms of managing diversity, but discover a newer, better way of managing people. With commitment and leadership at the top, and strict monitoring through goals and timetables, the emphasis is on right inputs (assumptions, values and beliefs), processes and outcomes. The company has created a database and conducts systematic research to check whether practise is aligned to policy, what accounts for gaps, if any and how such gaps need to be bridged. The various mechanisms in place will ensure that these are institutionalized. There is leadership, commitment and accountability at every level. Ultimately, the steady increase in bottom line, even in difficult business times, speaks volumes confirming the belief that workforce diversity and non-discrimination not only justifies social sensibility, but also makes immense business sense.

CHAPTER

2

building competency based HRM for success

M R CHANDRAMOULY*

* M R Chandramouly is Vice-President - Corporate HR with PRAXAIR (I) Ltd., Bangalore.

Background

This paper intends to make a general inquiry into competency movement, current competency-based models, and definitions. Here is an attempt to suggest the effectiveness of Competency Based HRM (CBHRM) is effective when it is underpinned by human values along with organization objectives and strategies. I am aware that more work remains to be done to validate competency utilization and identification of its value addition to Indian organizations.

What predicts performance? This has been the subject of scientific inquiry over centuries. Scientists have proposed a range of factors that determine behaviour and performance. These factors include aspects of physical shape of the head, brain weight, social class, birth order, handwriting, gender, religion, IQ, cultural heritage, and so on. Additional factors that have been used in attempt to predict performance in the workplace are technical skills, years of experience, education and personality traits.

In this background, a study of competencies began in the early 1970's. Researchers demonstrated that **behavioural traits and characteristics** are much more effective than **aptitude tests** in determining who is and is not successful in job performance.

Employers generally give as much attention to behavioural aspects as they do to the technical areas. In addition to the basic skills and formal education, non-academic skills are being widely influenced in deciding right candidate for a job, as can be seen by this survey data:

Employer's Recruiting Criteria In The US (1994-1997)

Employer's responses to the question: " After you have established your applicant pool and obtained information about potential employees, what characteristics or attributes are most critical in making your hiring decision".

The average responses are on a scale of 1 to 5 (1- not at all important; 5 =essential)

CHARACTERISTICS	1994	1997
Applicant's attitude	4.6	4.6
Applicant's communication skills	4.2	4.1
Previous employer references	3.4	3.9
Previous work experience	4.0	3.8
Industry based credentials	3.2	3.2
Years of completed schooling	2.9	2.9
Academic performance	2.5	2.5
Score on recruitment tests	2.5	2.3
Teacher recommendations	2.1	2.0
Experience/Reputation of school	2.4	2.0

(Source: " Connecting Work and School" A summary report on sectorial interviews – D Sapriro)

Psychologists wrote and thought about intelligence, in the beginning, when they focused on cognitive aspects such as memory and problem solving. Further researches recognized that the non-cognitive aspects were also important. During 1943, David Wechsler redefined intelligence as ' the aggregate or global capacity of the individual to act purposefully, to think rationally, and to deal effectively with this environment. Robert Thorndike wrote about 'social intelligence' during the same time. All these were largely ignored and faded away until 1983 Howard Gardner's writing about 'multiple intelligence' highlighting the importance of 'interpersonal' and 'intrapersonal' along with IQ related measurements. In 1956 AT&T used the 'assessment centre' concept, which included evaluation of non-cognitive as well as cognitive measures.

Competency-based methodology was pioneered by Hay-McBer company founder David McClelland, a Harvard University psychologist in the late 1960's. McClelland set out to define competency variables that could be used in predicting job performance and that were not biased by race, gender, or socioeconomic factors. His research helped identify performance aspects not attributable to a worker's intelligence or degree of knowledge and skill. McClelland's article, appearing in American Psychologist in 1973, entitled "Testing for Competence Rather Than for Intelligence," was a key point of development of the competency movement as an alternative to the intelligence testing movement.

McClelland's (1973) competency methodology can be summed up in two factors:

- "Use of criterion samples" or systematically comparing superior performing persons with less successful persons to identify successful characteristics and
- "Identification of operative thoughts and behaviours that are causally related to successful outcomes" or the best predictor of what persons can and will do in present and future situations is what they have actually done in similar past situations.

The emergence of globalization and consequential attributes like knowledge management, technological advances has ushered in a debate about the demand for higher levels of competencies. There is a growing acceptance on importance of competencies per se as a fulcrum for economic and personal growth.

Definition of Competency

In the business world today, there is some confusion over the definition of competency. The biggest confusion is between competencies and skills. Skills generally refer to the mastery of technique and knowledge that applies to a specific area or profession.

R Zemke (1982) (Training Vol 19 (5)) interviewed several experts in the field to determine " precisely what makes a competency" and he captures his finding thus:

"Competency, competencies, competency models, and competency-based training are all Humpty Dumpty words meaning only what the definer wants them to mean. The problem comes not from malice, stupidity or marketing avarice, but instead in some basic procedural and philosophical differences among those racing to define the concept and to set the model the way the rest of us will use competencies"

A **competency** refers to an individual's *demonstrated* knowledge, skills, behaviours, experiences, life views and values. Competencies are observable, behavioural acts that require a combination of all these attributes to execute. They are demonstrated in a job context and, as such, are influenced by an organization's culture and work environment.

Differences in definitions notwithstanding, Hendry and Maggio (1996) suggest that when competencies are linked to the broader goals of an organization, the following common elements emerge as outcomes of a comprehensive competency model:

- Identification of characteristics and behaviours that differentiate top performers from others in relation to their contribution to strategic objectives;
- Clarification, communication, assessment, and development of characteristics that focus individuals on core organization goals;

Description of skills, attitudes, traits, and behaviours *(and values)* that can be attached to pay, performance measurement, hiring criteria, training, organizational staffing, career development, and succession planning.

Example of Competency Definition

Competency: Customer Service Orientation

Responds to customer's needs in a manner that provides added value and generates significant customer satisfaction:

- Demonstrates a deep understanding of internal and external customers and their needs.
- Mobilises the appropriate resources to respond to customer's needs.
- Takes personal responsibility for customer satisfaction (e.g., focuses on value-added interactions).
- Builds credibility and trust with the customer through open and direct communication (e.g., uses effective listening skills, provides timely feedback, etc.).
- Ensures that customers believe their issues and concerns are given highest priority.

How Competencies are Useful for Organizations?

There is nothing magical about competencies. The competency paradigm is simply one way to break behaviour down into its component parts. Like any paradigm, it is useful to the extent that it helps explain reality, as we know it, and helps us influence and predict the reality of the future. Competencies are a useful concept to the extent that they can help explain why some people perform better than others do, to the extent that they help people improve their performance, and to the extent that they help people make decisions that will help them accomplish their objectives. When used effectively, the competency paradigm is a tonic for managers trying to improve their organization in these areas.

Competency based HRM Model

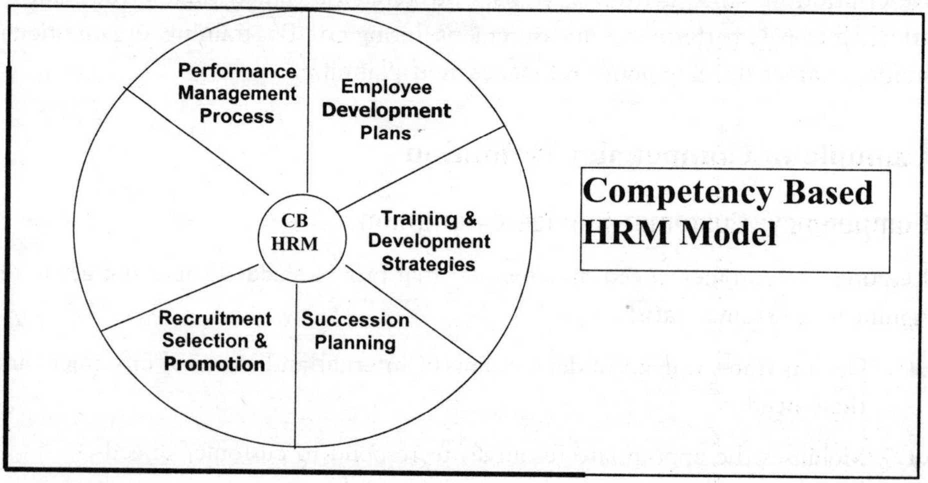

A study based on survey results from 292 members of the HR Benchmark Group reported positive impact in specific areas and outcomes when competencies supported corresponding HR systems. (Kevin W Cook and Paul Bernthal, DDI, Pittsburgh)

Organizations REPORTING OVERALL IMPROVEMENT	SYSTEMS SUPPORTED BY COMPETENCIES
30%	2 or fewer
57%	3
73%	4
84%	5
91%	6

	Advantages	Disadvantages
Competency Development	Links individual competencies to organizational strategies and goals.	Meaningless if an organization is not clear about its vision, strategies for their pursuit.
Cost of Development	Profiles to match position and person ensuring correct hiring.	Time consuming to administer stages of development, gap analysis, learning and assessment

While organizations have used the idea of competencies for over fifty years, the developing trend of the competency movement in India has resulted in a proliferation of definitions, tools, models and applications. All of which are not universally understood and applied. Organizations should consider expanding the use of competencies as a foundation for organizational change and improved performance for three reasons:

- The link between individual performance and organization performance drives competency-based learning systems. Competency development focuses on areas in which an individual, team or work group demonstrates outstanding performance and links them to strategic directions. Competency modelling can be a vehicle for moving organizations forward.
- Competency development is a highly participatory process. Professionals have the opportunity to identify the knowledge, skills and behaviours needed to get the best results as well as skills and functions that are no longer effective.
- The most important reason for organizations to consider competencies is that competency models are powerful decision-making tools. Professional organizations worldwide are finding competencies help make forward-looking human resource decisions by clarifying the knowledge, skills and behaviours needed in the future and by serving as a foundation upon which to build employee selection, training, professional development, performance appraisal, and succession planning.

Boyatzis (1982) used a contingency model of management effectiveness which postulated that the degree of overlap area (Best Fit) among the individual, job demands and organizational environment would predict effectiveness.

Predicting Organizational Effectiveness

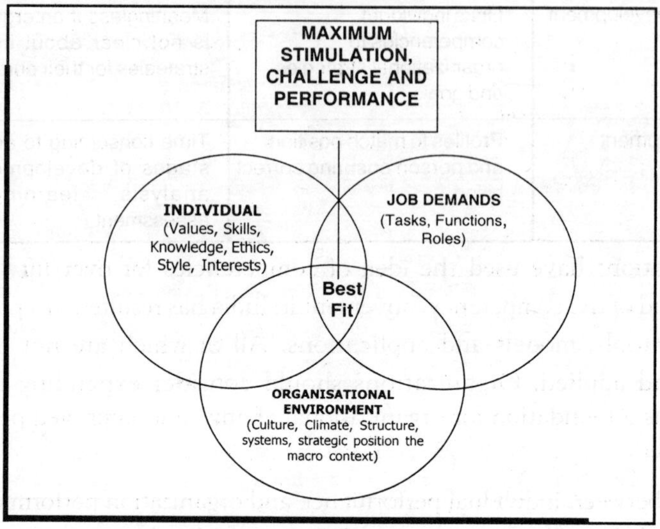

SOME GROUPS OF COMPETENCIES

Four Categories of Competencies

Leadership, which comes into play at all levels within the organization, needs to balance the four categories. Having all competencies in one category will NOT provide balance to behaviours and performance.

◢ PURPOSE. Competencies used to create/set and communicate / manage a strategic mission or vision; to chart the longer-term goals for the organization; to see the far horizon of possible scenarios and futures.
◢ PEOPLE. Competencies used in working with and managing / energizing others.
◢ PROCESS. Competencies used in managing the processes of organizations; how to organize; how to measure things; the practises and policies required to make things work; the management of

Contd...

	consequences; what gets rewarded and what gets punished; what needs to be done to get things done.
◢	PERSONAL. Competencies used in managing oneself while applying the Purpose, People and Process skills listed above, in order to achieve the above; needed to deploy oneself constructively against the business mission; perspectives used to show maturity of character and deportment in complex situations; characteristics that help insure against self-defeating behaviour.

a) Organizational Competencies

Those competencies, which are unique organizational factors of key competitiveness.

b) Job/Role Competencies

Those competencies which individuals are required to demonstrate to be effective in jobs and roles.

c) Essential Competencies

Those competencies, which are required, inherent, and fundamental for anyone in that job category.

d) Functional Competencies

Those competencies, which, along with the essential competencies, are necessary to perform a job at a particular band level.

COMPETENCY PROFILING

A competency profile generally, is composed of 5 to 10 competencies, but can include is as many or as few as are required to accurately reflect performance variations in the position. For instance, essential and functional competencies of an HR manager in a Fortune 500 company are given here,

Selected competencies for the position of HR Manager

ESSENTIAL COMPETENCIES	FUNCTIONAL COMPETENCIES
Action Oriented	Conflict Management
Listening	Organizational Agility
Peer Relationship	Priority Setting
Problem Solving	Timely Decision Making
Results	Understanding Others

Developing Competency Profile

There are two general approaches for developing competency profile. One is the 'top down approach'. Here competencies are picked based on strategic analysis of an organization's long term objectives and assessing those for particular position or class of positions. In the bottom-up approach, which appears to be in focus lately, competencies are identified from the existing best contributors mapped to the rest highlighting the gaps to fill up with developmental actions.

Recent surveys indicate widespread use of competency-based human resource models by banks, insurance companies, management consulting firms, technology companies, and transportation companies, retailing outlets, manufacturing industries. In India, competency based HR practices are used in companies like, SKF-Glaxo, Infosys, Wipro, GE, Phillips, Praxair and so on.

Survey by the American Compensation Association (1996) covering 217 organizations on use of competencies

Percentage of agreement on the effect of competencies on communicating valued behaviours and organizational culture	75% agreed
Percentage agreed on raising the bar of performance for all employees	59% agreed
Emphasizing people (rather than job) capabilities as away to gain competitive advantage	42% agreed
Encouraging cross-functional and team behaviour	34% agreed

Most competency programmes have been developed around the notion of organization developing a sustainable competitive advantage, larger profit margin over its competitors. Such competencies are intrinsic and must not lead themselves to easy duplication. Thus, simple imitation of another organization's success model is no guarantee of sustained competitive advantage for another organization unless their HR system attributes are unique and synergistic.

Suggestions

- Employer organizations alongwith the Government can establish interdisciplinary committees of successful managers/ leaders to advice on competency based HR movement considering the microeconomics of our country.
- There is a need to publish the different facets of the competency tool; how competencies are developed, applied, assessed; what competency options can be considered, what evidence would the quality standards like ISO, Six Sigma require to decide a broader definition and, standards of competencies required or organization and a dictionary of competencies.
- There is a need to look at what are the new competencies required, considering the current and future challenges in HRM. NHRD could conduct symposiums on global conceptions of competencies, on emotional intelligence and leadership excellence and further publish literature, applications in general HRM areas like recruitment, performance appraisal, succession planning, etc.

All areas of people and organizational effectiveness revolve around competencies. Competencies feed into all areas of people development.

Application of Competencies

Applying competencies to the different HR functions the organization gains greater benefits:

Job Profiles: Competencies create a consistent set of HR tools and common language for defining job skills and qualifications.

Recruiting: Competencies help in achieving consistency in hiring for the same jobs in different organizations, increasing the speed and reducing the cost of filling jobs, reducing turnover and training needs and balancing the need for behavioural as well as technical skills.

Development: Competencies help to focus development resources on the critical needs, which leads to improved performance, and to simplify development planning by using a common language and structure.

Workforce Planning: Competencies help to link job/organizational profiling with workforce assessment, identify performance and developmental gaps and determine required staffing actions (Deploy, Develop, Deselect, Differentiate People)

Organizational Development: Enhancing capability in people is the ultimate goal of HR work. Competencies help to increase people's skills and abilities by application to all the HR functions.

Each competency then, needs to be defined with demonstrated factors and activities. For instance, quality decision making must demonstrate analytical, creative and strategic thinking. Activity must show such incidents.

Building Competency Models

There are 3 widely used sources of data for competency models. 1. Focus group, panels or subject group experts; 2. Critical behaviour event interviews with superior performers and; 3. Generic competency terminologies and definitions.

Focused Groups/Panels follow a structured process to get particulars about the job and personal skills, attributes, knowledge, experience needed for effectiveness. They pose series of questions and capture the ideas and scan them through emerging changes in the organization, market and technology. They provide a forum for input about jobs and allow it to absorb inputs from different organizational constituencies with different stakeholders.

Behavioural event interviews involve in-depth probing of a significant number of broad events. It requires mastering a sophisticated probing strategy. They tape the conversations and transcribe so that it can be read and analysed. Of course, these steps significantly increase time and cost but these interviews have unique value. They can display how specific competencies are actually demonstrated by job incumbents.

Generic competency terminologies are available which are developed after extensive experience in competency modelling. They encounter the conceptual framework of generic competencies and behavioural indicators. Each competency could have 5 to 10 behavioural indicators. Competency dictionary provides a base for developing a straw model for organizations. It is further used to guide the analysis of behaviour event interviews.

One of the other types of building a model is a hybrid method, which involves using an intuitive approach to develop a prototype competency model and then collecting data and revising it based on the data analysis.

Much of the value of a competency model is underpinned from its behavioural descriptors. They are descriptions of behaviours and thought patterns that are hyphothesized to contribute to superior performance. The same descriptors are used to evaluate competency levels. There can be descriptors to create levels to which a competency is required in a particular job. It could be 'unskilled', 'skilled', 'overskilled' descriptors, which can be generated for each competency.

Clustering of Competencies

When an organization chooses among several competencies to develop its own model, it is important to know whether the competency characteristics are organized empirically and not theoretically. Each competency selected must be in the context of other competencies, which may affect each other closely and independently. In defining a set of competencies for a position, it is important to know which of the desired competencies are expected to be demonstrated together or associated with each other? (components of self-awareness competency are needed for self-management and a measurable component must be there to demonstrate consistency).

Each competency used may vary in settings and stimulus. It depends on the degree of minute and bigger component definition organizations put together. Cluster defined for each band of jobs, with a competency model must be related in some way, as parts of a whole and should not be a list of qualities.

Behavioural Descriptors Competency: Motivating Subordinates

Human Values Demonstrated

Trust, Positive Attitude, Equality, Compassion, Consistence, Simplicity, Truthfulness, Self Discipline, Non-Attachment, Gratitude

Skilled Definition: Can motivate many kinds of subordinates and team or project members; can assess each person's hot button and use it to get the best out of them; pushes tasks and decisions down; empowers others; invites input from each person and shares ownership and visibility; makes each individual feel their work is important; is someone people like working for and with.

Observable Behaviour: Inviting input/approachability. Patience with the unconverted and troubled people. Sharing visibility and credit. Able to predict what people will respond to. Pushing tasks/decisions down. Is very motivated himself/herself.

Unskilled Competency: Doesn't know what motivates others or how to do it; people under him/her don't do their best; not empowering and not a person many people want to work for, around or with; may be a one style fits all person, have simplistic models of motivation, or may not care as much as most others do; may be a driver just interested in getting the work done; may have trouble with people not like him/her; may be a poor reader of others, may not pick up on their needs and cues; may be judgmental and put people in stereotypical categories; intentionally or unintentionally demotivates others.

Overused: May not be good at building team spirit because of an emphasis on individuals; may be seen as providing inequitable treatment by treating each person individually; may not take tough stand when the situation calls for it; may wait too long for input; may be reluctant to assign work with tough deadlines.

ASSESSMENT CENTRE APPROACH TO COMPETENCY MAPPING

With the increasing demand for quality human resource, assessing the employee competency and building new competencies are becoming more critical. In the assessment centre approach, a team of trained assessors use variety of techniques, business games, in-basket, psychological tests, group discussions, presentations, and interviews for assessment. Assessment centres can provide a comprehensive standardized evaluation of competencies to the expectation of organizational objectives and they can contribute valuable information to a large number of functions in an organization.

Once a competency map has been developed and validated, it can be used as a tool to manage, evaluate, and develop employee performance; recruit those possessing right skills and compensate them based on demonstrated performances.

Conclusion

- A prime issue with competency based HRM, being relatively recent to India, has not yet been assessed. Hard data is not available to measure programme success and to validate underlying models, implicit or explicit.
- We seek to build competencies that predict more fulfilling lives since what we see today, are scams, cheating, short-term focus and suffering. Ironically, our understanding of individual personality and behaviour has advanced exceedingly from last 50 years.

COMPETENCY BASED INTERVIEWING FROM LEADERSHIP ARCHITECT MODEL

Interpersonal Savvy

Relates well to all kinds of people, up, down, and sideways, inside and outside the organization; builds appropriate rapport; listens; builds constructive and effective relationships; uses diplomacy and tact; truly values people; can diffuse even high-tension situations comfortably.

Sample Questions

- Have you ever had to negotiate with people you didn't like or didn't trust?
- What kind of network do you have laterally in the organization?
- Does your interpersonal style differ depending upon whom you're with?

Observations

- Observes, studies people.
- Observes own impact on others and changes behaviour accordingly.
- Anticipates reactions and objections.
- Drivers – Why does he/she act that way?
- Can keep personal feelings out of the transaction.
- Genuinely values people.

References

Raising the Bar: Using Competencies to Enhance Employee Performance. American Compensation Association (1996). Scotsdate.AZ:ACA.

The Competent Manager: A Model for Effective Performance, Boyatzis, R.E. (1982), New York, John Wiley and Sons.

Competency Based Performance: A Strategy for Organization, Dubois, DD (1993) Amherst MA: HRD Press Inc.

Competence at Work: Models for Superior Performance – L.M. Spencer and S.M Spencer 1993). New York: John Wiley & Sons.

Building Competency Models – Approaches for HR Professionals: Richard S Mansfield (1996).

I am also indebted to the extensive literature and research work done by Development Dimensions International and Lominger and Praxair Competency Programme and practical applications in countrywide workshops for internalizing competencies.

CHAPTER

3

executing projects of national importance using project aligned HRM model

a case study of POWERGRID

SRINIVAS R KANDULA*

* Srinivas R Kandula, is a doctorate in HRD from AHRD-XLRI and currently working with Power Grid Corporation of India.

The objective of present paper is two-fold: (i) to describe the linkages between business strategy and HRM and, role of HRM in project execution with the help of literature review and (ii) to present the live experience of POWERGRID in aligning HRM at different stages of project execution with the help of two successfully executed projects of national importance. With these objectives in view, the paper is organized into five parts such as (i) the linkages between business and HRM is discussed in part-1, role of HRM in project execution in part-2, brief about case study organization and projects executed in part-3, salient features of project aligned human resource management in part-4 and part-5 captures the key insights of this case study.

Business- HRM Alignment

Business aligned human resource management has gained prominence both in management literature and in its practise during the last and current decades. HRM professionals, however, approached the issue of integrating HRM with business strategy from different perspectives. These perspectives can be broadly classified into three: (i) a matching model that prescribes synchronizing design and implementation of HRM system with growth stages of organization, (ii) A proactive model that advocates integrating HRM at formulation of business strategy itself and (iii) A reactive model that suggests business strategy drives human resource strategy. A summary of these models/ major studies/ views / reflections of academicians, researchers and practitioners of HRM is illustrated at Table-A (see annexure-I).

Role of HRM in Execution of Projects

Project execution is one of the most important activities for any organization and in any business. The nature of these projects can be as big as erecting mega power, cement, petrochemical, fertilizer plants or laying optical fibre cables crisscrossing the country or developing an enterprise resource planning software to that of as small as constructing a mini housing complex or establishing a telecom terminal or writing a pay roll software programme. Human resource management has a significant role in effective execution of all such projects regardless of their size and complexity. A summary of views / studies/ reflections emphasizing the importance of HRM in project execution is given at Table-B (see annexure-I).

EXECUTING PROJECTS OF NATIONAL IMPORTANCE: A CASE STUDY OF POWERGRID

Power Grid Corporation of India Ltd., a Government of India enterprise was incorporated in the year 1989 with a mandate to create national power grid with an authorized share capital of Rs 5,000 crores. Within a span of a decade, POWERGRID emerged as the largest power transmission utility in the world. Today, the transmission network of the company encompasses 40000 circuit kilometres of transmission lines and transformation capacity of about 32000 MVA distributed over 65 sub stations crisscrossing length and breadth of the country. The turnover of the company stood at 2860 crores and profits at 760 crores for the year 2001-2002 financial year. POWERGRID has also diversified into telecom business with plans to invest about Rs. 10,000 crores and already created fibre optic cable network of 14000 kilometres with an investment of Rs 975 crores.

Brief About The Projects Of National Importance

In the year 1998, Power Grid Corporation of India was vested with the responsibility of executing two mammoth projects of national importance: (i) Unified Load Dispatch Communication Centre (ULDC) and (ii) East-South Back-to-Back HVDC Transmission System. The brief description of these projects is given below. The execution of these projects is a daunting task even to best of world-class engineers and managers, given the formidability of challenges. The challenges include (i) the newness of technology like HVDC and Communication System (ii) inadequacy of human resource competencies and (iii) geographical spread of operations.

- ***Unified Load Dispatch Centre (ULDC):*** Unified load dispatch & communication facilities are basic prerequisites for effective and efficient on-line management of regional and national power grids. In order to create this facility, Southern region of POWERGRID was given the responsibility of executing ULDC, benefiting four southern states with an investment of Rs 685 crores. This project involved setting up of 268 remote technical units and laying of 2311 kilometres of fibre optic cables. The execution of the project commenced in 1998 and commissioned successfully in January 2002.

East-South Back-to-Back HVDC Transmission System: This is the first trans-regional transmission system designed to transmit 2000MW of power from eastern region to southern region with an estimated cost of Rs 3,865 crores. The project execution commenced in January 2000 and scheduled to be commissioned in August 2002. The project comprises of 1370 kilometres long 500 KV bipolar HVDC transmission line traversing through the states of Orissa, Andhra Pradesh and Karnataka with terminal stations at Talcher and Kolar. It also comprises 700 kilometres long 400 KV transmission system beyond Kolar passing through the states of Tamilnadu and Karnataka with a new substation at Hosur and bay extensions at several existing sub stations. This is the largest transmission system undertaken by any power utility in the country and second largest in the world.

PROJECT ALIGNED HUMAN RESOURCE MANAGEMENT MODEL (PAHRM)

The challenges of executing these projects have been managed successfully using a systematic project aligned human resource system called 'Project Aligned Human Resource Management Model' (PAHRM) developed, tested, implemented, evaluated and systematized by POWERGRID. The model consists of five components (stages) such as: (i) Assessment of Human Resource Management Requirements, (ii) Audit of Human Resource Management System, (iii) Formulation of Human Resource Management Strategy, (iv) Implementation of Human Resource Management Strategy, (v) Evaluation of Human Resource Management Strategy. The schematic graph of this model is appended as Exhibit-I. These components are briefly presented here:

Assessment of Human Resource Management Requirements

In order to successfully erect and commission the projects well within the scheduled time adhering to budget sanctions and engineering specifications, human resource requirements were assessed on three vital parameters as indicated below:

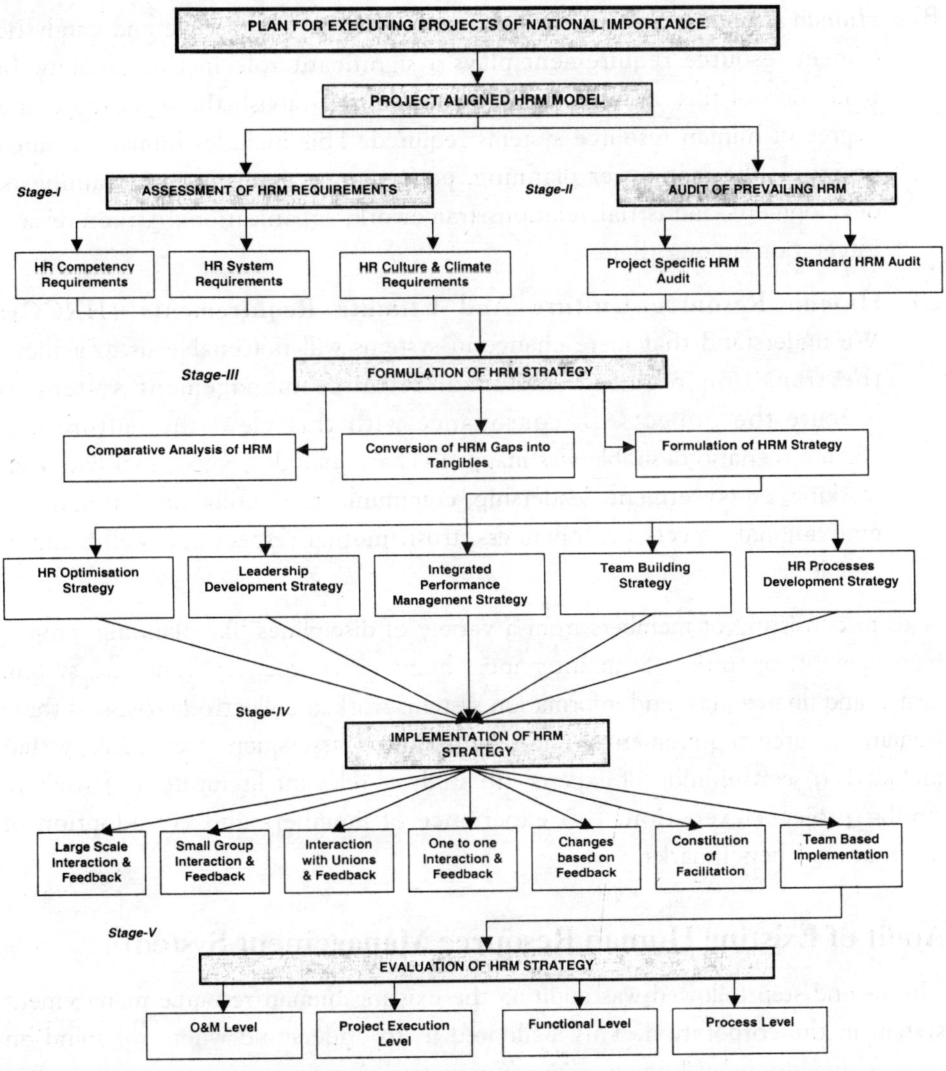

Exhibit I A Schematic Graph of Project Aligned Human Resource Management Model

A) ***Human Resource Competency Requirements (HRC):*** This process involves establishing the skills, competencies and knowledge required to execute the project. In other words, an inventory of required human competencies and trade skills was developed in relation to these specific projects.

B) ***Human Resource Systems Requirements (HRS)*:** Compatible and catalystic human resource requirement plays a significant role in this mission. In realization of this, an assessment was made to establish the type, scope and degree of human resource systems required. This includes human resource practises like manpower planning, performance management, training & development, industrial relations framework, organizational structure and integration among them.

C) ***Human Resource Culture And Climate Requirements (HRCC)*:** We understand that mere change in systems will not enable us to achieve the transition required in human resource management system to execute the projects. In consonance with this view, the culture and climate scenario desirable was mapped. These include components like team working, empowerment, leadership, communication, collaboration and soft motivational aspects i.e., openness, trust, mutual respect and well being of people.

A team consisting of members from a variety of disciplines like planning, project management, operation & maintenance, human resource, environment, system design and finance, law and information systems worked collectively to assess these human resource requirements. The team followed assessment methodology that included: (i) consultation of experts, (ii) study of relevant literature, (iii) study of similar projects execution, (iv) experience of members and (v) adoption of international benchmarks.

Audit of Existing Human Resource Management System

The second step followed was auditing the existing human resource management system in the corporation. This facilitated us to understand where we stand on various dimensions of human resource activities. A twin strategy was followed in implementation of this audit, as indicated below:

A) ***Project Specific HRM Audit (PSM)*:** The first strategy was auditing human resource on the three dimensions of human resource requirements: HRC, HRS and HRCC as explained in above.

B) ***Standard HRM Audit (STM):*** General audit of human resource on a standalone format using standard human resource audit instruments was carried out as second strategy.

Primary data collection techniques such as survey questionnaire, interviews and small group discussions and, secondary data collection techniques like study of written HR policies & regulations, HR database, relevant documents were used in auditing process. This resulted in generating valuable data, particularly the availability of human resource skills and competencies, the state of human resource system and culture aspects.

Formulation of Human Resource Management Strategy

This has been the most critical phase in the sequential activities performed to attain the objectives of project execution. Three major steps were followed in strategy formulation:

- ***Step-I: Comparative analysis of existing HRM and desirable HRM:*** A comparative study has been done to identify the gaps between existing HRM and desirable HRM on three standard parameters: Human Resource Competency, Human Resource System and Human Resource Culture & Climate based on the findings/ results of HRM requirement assessment and audit of prevailing HRM system as discussed in 4.1 and 4.2 above. The analysis contributed to locating the gaps in all the three areas.
- ***Step-II: Conversion of gaps into tangible practises:*** The gaps thus identified at Step-I was at macro level, like (i) skills gaps in commissioning of HVDC sub-station, (ii) absence of tight integration among HRM activities like training, performance appraisal, promotions etc., (iii) imbalance between value added human resource activities and service oriented human resource activities, (iv) culture and climate gaps like complacency in the place of achievement motivation, (v) powerlessness among managers, (vi) declining organizational commitment, (vii) individualized work preferences etc., These macro level issues were translated into tangibles in terms of HR policies & practises.
- ***Step-III: Formulation of HRM strategy:*** In order to bridge these HR policy and practise gaps, a five pronged strategy was followed as described below:

A) *Human Resource Optimization Strategy (HROS)*: The comparative analysis of assessm ent and audit reports revealed sub-optimal utilization of human resources in existing operations that include operation & maintenance of sub-stations and transmission lines in terms of quality and quantity of manpower. In other words, the studies clearly established over-manning of O&M projects and under-manning of construction projects. This over-manning happened due to the three-tier organizational hierarchical structure adopted in the corporation and implementation of a traditional manning norm. To overcome this problem, two action plans were formulated. Firstly, the middle tier of hierarchy was proposed for deletion. Secondly, manpower modules for O&M projects was remodeled to reduce manpower positioning from 11 to 7 in each sub-station. This predicted to save manpower to the tune of 195 employees in cumulative terms.

B) *Leadership Development Strategy (LDS)*: The survey also revealed a dominant perception of leadership as being only top management's arena. It was rightly realized that we need multiple leaders to execute projects

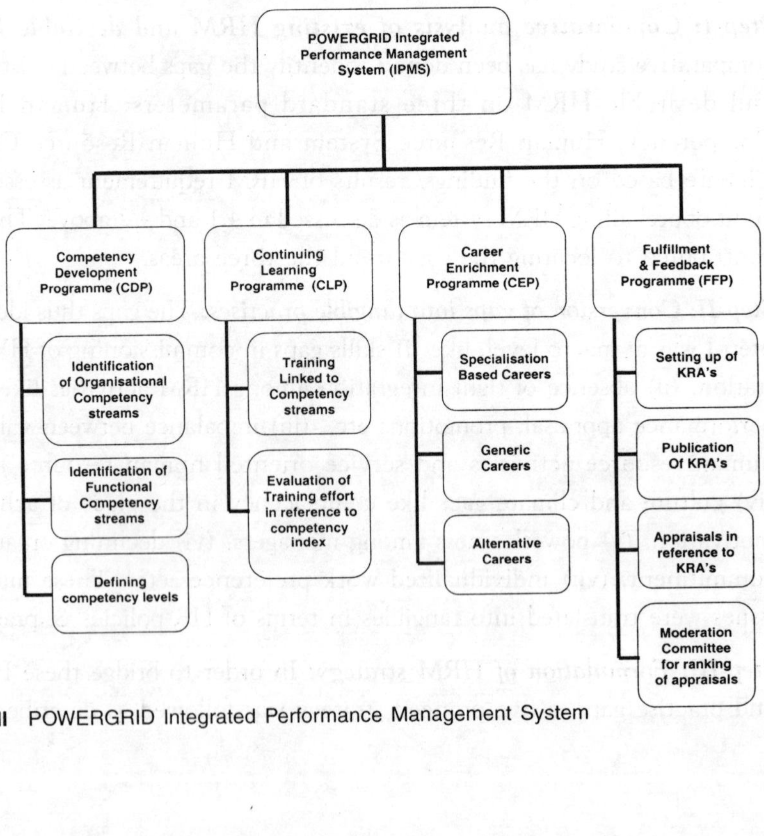

Exhibit II POWERGRID Integrated Performance Management System

of this scale. In pursuance to this, steps were planned to induce leadership at different levels that includes operating core, functional level, specialization level and regional level. The leadership development plan consisted classroom and field level training and is sharply linked to performance management.

C) *Integrated Performance Management Strategy (IPMS)*: The gaps reflected in this area were existence of performance appraisal, training and promotion as independent systems and many times as an end in themselves. Therefore, an integrated performance management strategy consisting four critical elements were covered. These are:

- Competency Development Programme (CDP)
- Continuous Learning Programme (CLP)
- Career Enrichment Programme (CEP)
- Fulfillment & Feedback Programme (FFP)

A pictorial graph of this integrated performance management strategy is appended as Exhibit-II.

D) *Team Building Strategy (TBS)*: The work orientation of projects involve inter dependence of tasks and empowerment of people to take decisions within minimum possible time. To achieve this, it was planned to build project execution teams at different locations. It was also planned to train them on problem-solving and inter- personal skills.

E) *Human Resource Processes Development Strategy (HRPDS)*: The audit report found weak organizational commitment and complacency among human resource. It also pointed out unhealthy group dynamics and reluctance of people to take risks and move to other functional areas. The project execution and remodeled manpower modules required people to be redeployed. In this backdrop, a series of one to one meetings with top managers and small group meetings were planned to resolve these issues and to build salutary work culture.

Implementation of Human Resource Management Strategy

It is easier said than done. We understand the challenges involved in implementation of this five-pronged strategy. However, we believed that successful execution of these projects is sheerly contingent upon effective implementation of this project aligned human resource strategy. In other words, the premise was success of human resource strategy is just equivalent to successful execution of two projects. A series of implementation mechanisms were drawn that include:

A) ***Large-scale interactions involving all the employees:*** Executive Director of the region used the occasion of annual company day to unfold the proposed project aligned human resource management strategy.

B) ***Small group meetings:*** A group of managers were trained as resource persons using project review and operation review meetings as platforms on the new project aligned human resource management strategy.

C) ***Meetings with trade union office bearers at regional and substation levels:*** Meetings were held with union office bearers to transmit the details of proposed human resource strategy.

D) ***One to one meetings:*** One to one basis meetings were conducted and facilitated by managers trained as resource persons to impress upon the importance and essential features of this human resource strategy.

E) ***Feedback incorporation:*** Feedback received at all these interactions was analysed and, changes wherever required incorporated. In general, there was agreement on majority of the issues and in regard to new human resource strategy and practises.

F) ***Constitution of facilitation team:*** A team, steered by head of the region and facilitated by the author of this paper was constituted to facilitate the implementation of human resource strategy and also monitor the progress of implementation.

G) ***Simultaneous implementation of human resource strategy:*** Using teams, both physical and virtual teams, initiated by head of the region and owned by all the employees, the new human resource strategy was implemented simultaneously that included (i) massive redeployment of manpower from O&M stations to construction projects, (ii) competency development through training & development, (iii) mentoring, (iv) leadership development at all levels, (v) integration and rationalization of appraisals, promotions, (vi) mutual setting of performance targets flowing from project targets, (vii) top management standing as an example demonstrating virtues of organizational commitment and (viii) practising open communication etc., In this process, teams were used as medium of change as well as target of change.

Evaluation of Human Resource Management Strategy

Though, the facilitation team provided feedback on continuous basis based on their observations, it was felt necessary to carry out a systematic evaluation of human resource management strategy on completion of one year of its implementation. Pursuantly, a four level evaluation was done as briefly described below:

A) ***O & M level evaluation:*** The O&M level evaluation was done to understand the effectiveness of human resource management strategy in terms of line availability and financial effectiveness. The evaluation found that it resulted in significant positive gains to the region that included (i) system availability stood at 99.71 percent against the target of 98.25 percent (ii) satisfaction of employees reflected in zero man hours lost and harmonious industrial relations, lastly and more importantly the report highlighted that (iii) **redeployment of 195 employees to outside O&M set up resulted in recurring saving of Rupees 4 crores annually.**

B) ***Project level evaluation:*** The parameters adopted for evaluation of human resource strategy at project level includes: (i) achievement of project execution targets, (ii) availability of human skills and competence in execution of projects and (iii) satisfaction of employees. The evaluation revealed that implementation of project aligned human resource management strategy has strong positive correlation to:

- Commissioning of ULDC Project as per the schedule.
- Progress of East-South Back-to-Back Transmission system execution ahead of the schedule by nearly 6 months.
- No skill and competency shortage in execution of the projects.
- Employees' satisfaction with new human resource strategy.

C) ***Functional level evaluation:*** Evaluation was also conducted to understand the skill and competency availability in each functional area. The feedback was sought from each employee to the effect how the new human resource strategy implementation affected them in terms of functional competency. Large number of employees felt that this helped them to chart their competency plan and acquire skills in an evolutionary manner. Functional heads also expressed that new HR strategy strengthened the functional competency. **This may be for the first time that skills and competencies were build internally to execute such mega high-tech projects.**

D) ***Process level evaluation:*** This was done using survey and interview methodology eliciting perceptions of employees. The analysis of data highlighted that new human resource strategy contributed for (i) building mutual bonds among employees, (ii) increased feeling of ownership, (iii) knowledge empowerment, (iv) enriched jobs (v) improved communication and (vi) instilled a sense of achievement and meaning in the work.

CONCLUSION

It is named as Project Aligned Human Resource Management Model (PAHRM) because the model contributed for execution of two projects of national importance successfully and this credit largely is attributable to people and the model that facilitated. The implementation of this model also contributed to gain following insights:

A) The value of human capital gets multiplied when human resource policies and practises are aligned with company's vision, mission and objectives.

B) Human resource policy & practise should be sharply aligned with project management at formulation of project execution strategy itself. This contributes not only to commission projects successfully within the time and budget schedules but also creates value to human resource function.

C) The focus of human resource management needs to be shifted from maintenance & administration to strategic role in which operational aspects (implementation plan) are in-built.

D) Involvement of all people in the organization is a prerequisite for development and systematic implementation of PAHRM. Human resource managers have to become missionaries to realize the model in practise.

E) The emphasis on human resource management practises needs to be altered from collective bargaining to performance management.

F) The core and ancillary mechanisms of the model engaged in audit, assessment and implementation of PAHRD should be evaluated at regular intervals to gauge their efficacy and to incorporate necessary timely changes.

Project aligned human resource management model could be applied and replicated in all types of organizations. This is because the basic methodology followed in diagnosis, development, implementation of human resource strategy and its evaluation has universal applicability.

REFERENCES

Ackerman, K.F. (1986). A Contingency Model of HRM Strategy: Empirical Research Findings Reconsidered. *Management Forum*, 9 (6), pp. 65-83.

Armstrong, M. and H. Murlis (1991). *Reward Management: A Handbook of Remuneration Strategy and Practise* (2nd ed.). London: Kogan Page.

Arthur, M. (1994). Rover Managers Learn to Take a Back Seat. *Personnel Management*, 26(1), pp. 58-63.

Balkan, D.B. and I.R. Gomez-Mejia (1990). Matching Compensation and Organizational Strategy. *Strategic Management Journal*, 11(2), pp. 153-69.

Bartel, A. (1989). Formal Employee Training Programmes and their Impact on Labour Productivity: Evidence from a Human Resource Survey. *NBER Working Paper*, Series No.3026. Cambridge, Massachusetts: National Bureau of Economic Research.

Beatty, C. and C.D. Schneier (1988). Strategic Performance Appraisal Issues. In R.S. Schuler, S.A. Youngblood, and V.L. Huber (Eds.). *Readings in Personnel and Human Resource Management*, (3rd ed.) St. Paul: West Publishing, pp. 256-266.

Beaumont, P.B. (1993). *Human Resource Management*. London: Sage.

Becker, B.E. and C.A. Olson (1986). The Impact of Strikes on Shareholder Equity. *Industrial and Labour Relations Review*, 39(4), pp. 425-458.

Beer, M. and Spector, Bert (Ed.). (1985). *Readings in HRM*. New York: The Free Press.

Bluedorn, A. (1982). The Theories of Turnover: Causes, Effects, Meanings. In S. Bacharah (Ed.), *Research in Sociology of Organization*, *pp*. 75-128. Greenwich, Connecticut: JAI press.

Buller, Paul (1988). Successful Partnerships: HR and Strategic Planning at Eight Top Firms. *Organizational Dynamics*, Autumn, pp. 27-43.

Carrol, S.B. (1987). Business Strategies and Compensation Systems. In D.B. Balkin and L.R. Gomez-Mejia (Eds.), *New Perspectives in Compensation,* pp. 343-355. Englewood Cliffs, New Jersey: Prentice-Hall.

Chakravarthy, B.S. and E.J. Zajac (November 1984). Diversification Strategy. *Planning Review,* pp. 43-51.

Costa Giovanni, Arnaldo Camuffo (1993). Strategic Human Resource Management: Italian Style. *Sloan Management Review,* Winter, pp. 59-67.

Davis, S. (December 1981). Relating Human Resources Management to Business Strategy (summary). *Proceedings of the Human Resource Policy Institute,* pp. 3-5. Virginia: HRPI Publication.

Fabi, B. and N. Petterson (1992). Human Resource Management Practises in Project Management. *International Journal of Project Management,* 10(2), pp. 81-88.

Flamholtz, E.G. (1985). *Human Resource Accounting,* (2nd ed.,) San Francisco: Jossey-Bass.

Gerstein M. and H. Reisman (1983), Strategic Selection: Matching Executives to Business Conditions. *Sloan Management Review, 24*(2), pp. 1-18.

Gullett, Ray C. (November-December 1972). Personnel Management in the Project Environment. *Personnel Administration,* pp. 17-22.

Guzzo, R.A., R.D. Jettie and R.A. Katzell (1985). The Effect of Psychologically Based Intervention Programmes in Worker Productivity: A Meta Analysis. *Personnel Psychology,* 38(4), pp. 275-291.

Harrison, F.L. (1981). *Advanced Project Management.* England: Gower Publishing.

Harvey, I.J. (1983). Effective Planning for Human Resource Development. *Personnel Administrator,* 28(10), pp. 45-52.

Hendry, C. and A. Pettigrew (1986). The Practise of Strategic Human Resource Management. *Personnel Review,* 15(3), pp. 3-8.

Hendry, C. and A. Pettigrew (1992). Patterns of Strategic Change in the Development of Human Resource Management. *British Journal of Management,* 3(3), pp. 137-156.

Holzer, H.J. (1987). Hiring Procedures in the Firm: Their Economic Determinants and Outcomes. In M.M. Kleiner et al. (Eds), Human Resources and the Performance of the Firm, pp. 84-92. Washington: BNA Press.

Huselid, M.A. (1995). The Impact of Human Resource Management Practises on Turnover, Productivity, and Corporate Financial Performance. *Academy of Management Journal,* 38(4), pp. 635-672.

Ichniowski, C. (1990). Human Resource Management Systems and the Performance of U.S. Manufacturing Businesses. *NBER Working Paper, Series* No.3449. Cambridge, Massachusetts: National Bureau of Economic Research.

Katz, H.C., T.A. Kochan and J.H. Keefe (1983). *Industrial Relations and Productivity in the US Automobile Industry.* Washington, DC: Brookings Institution.

Katz, H.C., K T.A. Kochan and K.R. Gobeille (1985). Industrial Relations Performance, Economic Performance, and QWL Programmes: An Interplant Analysis. *Industrial and Labour Relations Review,* 37(3), pp. 3-17.

Kelly, T. (January 1989), Strategic Partnerships in HRM. *Personnel Administrator,* pp. 76-82.

Lengnick-Hall, Cynthia A. and Mark L. Lengnick-Hall (1988). Strategic Human Resources Management: A Review of the Literature and a Proposed Typology. *Academy of Management Review,* 13(3), pp. 454-470.

Leontiades, M. (1982). Choosing the Right Manager to Fit the Strategy. *Journal of Business Strategy,* 2(2), pp. 58-69.

Linkow, Peter (May 1985). HRD at the Roots of Corporate Strategy. *Training & Development Journal,* pp. 85-87.

Migliore, R.H. (1982). Linking Strategy, Performance and Pay. *Journal of Business Strategy,* 3(1), pp. 90-94.

Miles, R.E. and C.C. Snow (1984). Designing Strategic Human Resource Systems. *Organizational Dynamics,* 13(1), pp. 36-52.

Miller, P. (1987). Strategic Industrial Relations and Human Resource Management: Distinction, Definition and Recognition. *Journal of Management Studies,* 24(4), pp. 347-362.

Miller, P. (February 1989). Strategic HRM: What it is and What it isn't. *Personnel Management,* pp. 46-51.

Niehaus, Richard J. and K.F. Price (Ed.) (1991). *Bottom Line Results from Strategic Human Resource Planning.* New York: Plenum Press.

Ostroff, C. (21 June 1995), *Human Resource Management: Ideas and Trends in Personnel.* Issue No.36, CCH Inc.

Peck, Sharon R. (1994). Exploring the Link Between Organizational Strategy and the Employment Relationship: The Role of Human Resources Policies: *Journal of Management Studies,* 31(15), pp. 715-736.

Pfeffer, J. (1994). *Competitive Advantage Through People: Unleashing the Power of the Workforce.* Boston: Harvard Business School Press.

Randolph, Alan W. and Barry Z. Posner (1988). *Effective Project Planning & Management.* Englewood Cliffs, New Jersey: Prentice-Hall.

Reeser, Clayton (1969). Some Potential Human Problems of the Project Form of Organization. *Academy of Management Journal,* 12(4), pp. 462-466.

Schuster, F.E. (1986). *The Schuster Report: The Proven Connection Between People and Profits.* New York: John Wiley & Sons.

Sheutub, Abraham, J.F. Bard and Shlomo Globerson (1994). *Project Management.* Englewood Cliffs, New Jersey: Prentice-Hall.

Sonnenfield, J.A. and M.A. Peiperl (1988). Staffing Policy as a Strategic Response: A Typology of Career Systems. *Academy of Management Review,* 13(4), pp. 588-600.

Sweet, J. (1982). How Manpower Development Can Support Your Strategic Plan. *Journal of Business Strategy,* 3(1), pp. 77-81.

Tichy, N., C.J. Fombrun, and M.A. De Vanna (1982). Strategic Human Resources Management. *Sloan Management Review,* 23(2), pp. 47-64.

Waterman, Robert H. (1994). *What America Does Is Right.* New York: Norton.

Annexure-I

Table-A

LINKAGES BETWEEN BUSINESS STRATEGY AND HRM

Author(s)/Researcher(s)	Views/Reflections/Research Findings
Davis (1981)	Used product life cycle to explain human resource management from a strategic perspective.
Harvey (1983); Leontiades (1982); Migliore (1982); Sweet (1982); Gerstein and Reisman (1983)	Described human resources strategy as developing a match between certain strategic and organizational conditions and certain specified aspects of human resource processes and skills.
Tichy et al., (1982); Ackerman, (1986); Miller, (1989)	There is a widespread belief that HRM is the dependant variable and business strategy, the independent variable in this relationship. The view is that HRM should in some sense follow business strategy
Bluedorn (1982)	Extremely high or low levels of employee turnover reduced profits.
Katz, Kochan and Keefe (1983)	Innovative work practises like increased managerial discretion in allocation of labour hours, job transfers & lay-off improved productivity.
Chakravarthy and Zajac (1984)	Found relationship between strategy and incentive compensation system.
Miles and Snow (1984)	Human resource practises are part of the systems and processes that are expected to be consistent with strategy. Presumably, HR policies influence employee behaviour. If different employee behaviours are required to implement different strategies, then HR policies should systematically vary with organizational strategy.
Beer and Spector, (1985); Hendry and Pettigrew (1986); Miller (1987)	Approaching HRM from a business strategy perspective, they argue that HRM will be effective only when human resource strategy is integrated with business strategy.
Linkow (1985)	The HRD department has a two-fold role to play in strategy development. It should be involved in formulating corporate strategy; then it should develop its own strategy consistent with the strategy of the organization.
Flamholtz (1985)	The economic returns from investment in human resources policy and practises are substantial.
Guzzo, Jette and Katzell (1985)	HR management interventions involving training, goal setting etc. had a significant positive effect on productivity.

Katz, Kochan and Gobeille (1985)	Effective industrial relation system (operationalized as fewer grievances, disciplinary actions and lower absenteeism) increased product quality.
Becker and Olson (1986)	Strikes have a substantial negative effect on shareholder equity.
Schuster (1986)	Use of greater number of HR interventions like assessment centres, flexible work schedules, gain sharing and organizational development had a substantial and positive effect on firm performance.
Carroll (1987)	Compensation systems were designed to fit business strategies
Holzer (1987)	Some form of recruiting systems increased productivity.
Buller (1988)	Organizations are realizing that the success of their long-range planning and strategic approaches rests on corresponding analyses and planning by human resources.
Beatty and Schneier (1988)	Performance management systems were designed to help managers assess and manage strategic performance.
Lengnick-Hall and Lengnick-Hall (1988)	Found the links between human resources policies as a whole with an organization stay in the product life cycles.
Sonnenfield and Peiperl (1988)	Found links between staffing system and strategic orientation.
Kelly (1989)	Business strategy would give direction to HR activities, and HR issues, internal and external, would be considered in the business planning process.
Bartel (1989)	Training programs increased productivity between 11% and 18%.
Balkan and Gomez-Mejia (1990)	Found association between organizational strategy and compensation policy in a survey of HR managers.
Ichniowski (1990)	Found a positive association between the firms' HR management practices and organizational productivity.
Niehaus and Price (1991)	To remain competitive in a constantly changing environment, many organizations are making human resources a significant part of their long-range business and strategic planning.
Armstrong and Murilis (1991)	Reward management strategies and policies are driven by strategic changes occurring inside the organization.
Hendry and Pettigrew (1992)	The upshot is that matching is not the issue. Rather, it is a question of being in sense to the opportunities and constraints afforded for the development of HRM that emerge out of complex patterns of strategic and structural change.

Beaumont (1993)	The central aspect in the human resource management literature is of a strategic focus. The need for (i.) human resource policies and practises to be consistent with overall business strategy and (ii.) the need for individual components of a human resource management package to reinforce each other while the individual components of the package should primarily emphasize team work, flexibility, employee involvement and organizational commitment.
Costa Giovanni and Camuffo (1993)	Human resources practises contribute to strategy development and implementation
Waterman (1994)	Provided an important insight on the connection between strategy and effective management of people; he says people are the strategy.
Peck (1994)	Found relationship between organization strategy and HR. He also concluded that strategy/HR links are stronger in effective organizations than ineffective ones.
Pfeffer (1994)	Found a significant correlation between high commitment work practises such as employment security, high wages, employee ownership, information sharing, participation and empowerment, cross training and redesign of jobs and organization performance.
Arthur (1994)	Empirically identified the mills with commitment system, which had higher productivity and lower employee turnover than those with control systems.
Huselid (1995)	Found a significant correlation between implementation of high performance work practises & company's financial performance.
Ostroff (1995)	Developed a HR quality index. Firms that score higher in the HR quality index consistently outperform firms with a lower index in four financial measures: market/book value ratio, productivity (i.e. sales/employees) market value and sales.

Table-B

ROLE OF HRM IN PROJECT EXECUTION

Author(s)/Researcher(s)	Views/Reflections/Research Findings
Reeser (1969)	Identified five HR problems that exist in project organizations viz: (i) Anxiety about possible loss of employment, (ii) Frustration with ambiguity of authority, (iii) Confusion due to lack of formal procedures & regulations, (iv) Employees tend to be less loyal to the organization and (v) Employees perceive all assignments as temporary and adhoc
Gullett (1972)	Identified five major HR challenges in Project execution. These are: (i) Staffing levels are more variable, (ii) Performance evaluation is more complex and more subject to error, (iii) Wage & salary grades are more difficult to maintain as job descriptions are less valued, (iv) Training & development is more important in projects but least appreciated and (v) Morale problems are potentially greater.
Harrison (1981)	Effective project systems and good human relations systems are both necessary for good performance of projects, but neither is sufficient on its own. If one has good human relations in a project, reasonable performance can be obtained, whereas, if people are antagonizing each other, good project performance will never be achieved, no matter how good the project systems are.
Randolph and Posner (1988)	Observe that time and again studies reveal that projects fail because of mismanagement of people. They suggest four HR interventions such as: (i) Empower people on project, (ii) Ensure effective communication, (iii) Build great teams and (iv) Inspire a shared vision
Fabi and Patterson (1992)	Established that education and training of employees, proper performance assessment, job specifications and job security have special significance in the management of projects.
Sheutub, Bard and Globerson (1994)	The importance of teamwork is very high in managing the projects where employees from many disciplines join to perform multi-functional tasks.

CHAPTER

4

human resource management education at the heart of business

G PANDU NAIK AND K JANARDHANAM *

* G.Pandu Naik and K. Janardhanam are with Canara Bank School of Management Studies, Bangalore University, Bangalore.

India is undergoing rapid changes in socio-cultural and politico-economic fronts in the past 10 years. The changes are more accelerated in the economic front with the onset of liberalization, privatization and globalization since early 1990s. Till then, 42 years of independent India since 1947 was run like a socialistic regime with public sector enterprises acquiring priority. Production of goods and services were controlled by the State, including the imports and exports. Emphasis was laid on indigenization, localization and self reliance. These measures have brought prosperity in some sectors of the economy. For example the green revolution which changed India from food scarce to food surplus country. The dairy development in cooperative sector started with Gujarat has eradicated the shortage of milk and milk products. But for any country to bank on its own resources and knowhow for continuous development has limitations. This is the case with India too. It was able to achieve progress in select areas like agriculture and animal husbandry on its own for nearly 40 years after independence and then began the stagnation and decline. The main thrust for self reliance was born out of the enslaved life that we lived in the hands of colonial Europeans who entered India as traders and thereafter ruled us for nearly 400 years.

In India the privatization, liberalization and globalization process which started in 1990 has made tremendous impact on the society. National economy is moving towards global economy. Movement of capital, technology and labour from one country to the other is becoming easier day by day. State control is being relaxed and the economy is passing towards market controlled system. The gap between the rich and poor is widening but it is equally true that more and more people are becoming rich and richer. Though it is said to be survival of the fittest in the market economy, it is also true of the Government mobilizing more revenue for social security benefits of the needy poor. Indigenous R&D may be down but cheap transfer of superior technology is made possible. Government subsidies on the weaker sections of the society is down and tax holidays for those who create wealth is on. But the better side of this story is also true that we as an emerging economy have become a launching pad of the world's most successful enterprises. The benefits of information technology revolution is no more confined to the urban elite. Cable televisions, wireless phones, satellite weather forecasting, hybrid seeds and scientific soil testing are also benefiting the rural masses. The land of the agriculturists or the grains they produce have all acquired better market value today. Finally, the people at large are benefiting by best of products and services at competitive prices. Manufacturing sectors are driven more by machines and more and more people are employed in the service sectors. In this fast changing economic order the most important beneficiary is the customer. He dictates how a product has to be designed or how a service is to be delivered at competitive prices. Those who listen to him are most likely to survive than who does not.

THE CHANGING ROLE OF HUMAN RESOURCE MANAGEMENT

The impact of liberalization, globalization and privatization has tremendously changed the nature, role, concept and significance of human resource management in the Indian corporate world. With the national economy moving towards global economy the rules of the game have changed. Fixed working is being replaced by flexible working. Manual worker is down and skilled worker is up. Physical working is less and mental working is more. People are moving from the traditional stable jobs to work focussed contractual jobs. One time learning is no longer enough and continuous learning has become the necessity. Those who were looking for job opportunities locally, are now trying for the global opportunities. Retrenchment of workers is not much of an issue today but retention is. Large unskilled work force is vanishing and small groups of skilled knowledge workers are emerging. Proletariat classes can no longer be classified enmass as lower middle classes. The rules of wealth creation has converted very many workers into millionaires. Real work place concepts are drifting towards virtual work places. People can work right from their homes or from anywhere in the World. Many of the service conditions like pay and allowances are regulated by market forces than by labour laws. Private sector enterprises are slowly moving ahead of state owned public sectors. There was a time of hanging 'No Vacancy' boards in front of every factory, but now marketing of HR policies is the new concept to attract and retain the talented persons. Hitherto, recruitment of persons was dependent upon several factors like Government norms, management bias and social background of the candidates. But now it is the skill and competency based choice, irrespective of the religion, caste, language or place of birth of the candidate.

The role and relevance of the trade union is down and competent people are preferring to work directly with the trustworthy companies. Labour dispute and labour relation is no more a serious issue. Maintenance functions like preparing payrolls or submitting statutory returns can be outsourced at lower prices. More time and attention is being invested in helping the employees to contribute their best. HR departments are not functioning in isolation, rather the HR goals are being aligned with business goals of the organization.

Those who were working for the employers are now looking for starting their own ventures even at the cost of sacrificing high paid jobs. Manual procedures and paper based personnel departments are moving towards paper less computer network store houses of knowledge. Competent people from anywhere in the world can be employed and skillful Indians can also be employed overseas. Development of new technologies like networking, e-mail, internet, video conferencing, mobile phone etc. is enabling us to generate, share, transform or transfer the knowledge much faster than ever before. Employees are no more at the mercy of HR Managers. They have rather occupied the centrestage as customers of HR department. Thus, success of a HR Manager and his department depends upon the employee satisfaction and well being. In the knowledge driven contemporary enterprises, HR Managers are expected to show the tangible results of their policies and practices by retaining and motivating the best talented professionals. The HR Managers who could not keep employee turnover below 25% are even asked to resign by their companies.

The Input to HR Profession

The people entering the HR profession are from varied backgrounds. Those who do the Master of Social Work (MSW), Master of Business Administration (MBA), Master of Industrial Psychology, Master of Public Administration and engineers are all allowed into HR profession. Those who do the post graduate diploma of 6 months to 2 years duration and the law graduates are also entering this profession. The type of subjects taught in each of these courses differ significantly. For example, in social work, emphasis is given more on peoples well-being without looking into the business perspectives of HRM. The MBAs are pro-business without much concern to the people responsible for running the business. Public Administration people, learn issues related more to Government administration than business. Industrial psychologists concentrate on behavioural issues in organization, without considering the other aspects. Law graduates look at rule of law and legal compliance. The short duration (less than 2 years) diploma holders are not able to cover many important subjects of relevance due to time constraints. Instead of getting the courses curtailed accelerated learning need be encouraged. It is therefore, necessary to develop a common entrance test for all those who want to work in HRM, if not a common syllabus for all the above courses. And to oversee the qualitative education in HRM, national level council should be established. HRM education has got to be timely, relevant, purposeful and continuously updated looking into the changing needs of the employing organizations.

THE ROLE AND FIELD OF HRM

HR professionals at present are serving in different roles like Personnel Officer, Welfare Officer, HRD Officer, Labour Law Officer, Industrial Psychologist, Employee Counsellor, Training Officer, Recruitment Officer and Administrative Officer. Therefore, it is essential to introduce certain common subjects like importance of human resources for the sustainable success of business and the need of successful business for the survival of human resources.

HR professionals are required to work in different industries like banking, hospitality, software, manufacturing, plantations, mining etc. They also have to work in various sectors like private, public, cooperative, multinationals etc. Therefore, the course content for the HRM must invariably touch in deep, the nature and role of HRM in different industries and also in different sectors. Modern organizations are looking for competent persons of integrity who can lead the work force towards progress. HRM education must therefore be such to prepare the students as principle centred leaders with strategic vision.

Indian industries having multi-locational production facilities is not a new phenomenon. But, they were normally confined to a State or in different States within the country. Now, the wind of liberalization has changed the pattern, and more and more Indian companies are opening their business establishments in foreign countries. Therefore, HRM education should include international HR practices, procedures, prospects and legal requirements with respect to important countries. For example, those who have to work in the United States of America as HR Managers must follow the procedures of Affirmative Action programme and the equality provisions under the Federal Civil Rights Act 1964.

RE-ORIENTING THE HRM COURSES

More and more companies are expecting HR professionals to outsource the routine maintenance functions and devote more attention to the employee's well-being to retain the talented employees. HRM education must therefore, incorporate detailed behavioural science courses involving organizational behaviour, personality theories, emotional intelligence, methods of working with people, counselling psychology, psychometric testing etc.

There is a deep feeling in the minds of many corporates, that HR departments always remain isolated from the business concerns of the company and work like paramedical staff of an hospital. It is therefore, important to teach in the HRM courses, the importance of aligning HR goals to business goals of the organization. HRM students must be taught to work as active strategists of business, than sitting like irrelevant entities.

In the contemporary customer driven business organizations, HR departments can no more ignore the value of customer in business. The employees of the organization are the customers of HR departments. If the needs and aspirations of the employees are handled properly with a human touch, they will be happy to contribute their best for the success of the company. This will also help in retaining the talented employees for organizational progress. Further it is not a highly technical job to know the needs and problems of external customers of the company. Knowledge of customer expectations will help HR professionals to evolve appropriate learning initiatives for the employees so that they can effectively function in retaining and enhancing the customer base. It is time the HRM courses which hitherto remained aloof from teaching customer service management to, now look at this issue realistically. This will not only benefit the organization but the relevance of HRM professionals in business would be clearly visible.

ENLARGING AND ADDING THE RELEVANT SUBJECTS

The very nature of half-feeding certain subjects require re-examination and enhancement. For example, if we take the teaching of law for HRM courses, it is limited to labour law. An employee is appointed in an organization by contract of employment but law of contract is not taught. An employee has family but family law is not taught and HR people do not know handling a family dispute, income tax has to be deducted but do not know law of taxation. And in the knowledge intensive industries who will handle issues like intellectual property rights, patents and copyrights, if HR professionals do not know about it. It is therefore, necessary for the existing courses to be expanded to meet the changing demands of the HR departments. There are certain other subjects which are very important for the success of HRM, but not taught. For example, costing and accountancy. If HR professionals have to work out the cost involved in appointing 10 new supervisors or to start a canteen or to understand the company's balance sheet, knowledge of costing and accountancy is essentially required.

Looking at the Contemporary Issues and Practices

Though it is said that knowledge of history guides us to the future to some extent, what is significant for the present is important. HRM courses should include the contemporary HR practices, concepts and issues. For example, employee retention strategies like stock option plans, knowledge management programmes, people capability maturity models, 360 degree appraisals, HR audit, work place wellness etc.are important issues today needing additional importance. Some existing courses need modification or refinement. For example, in the discipline management, the companies wanted to have strong internal walls and external compounds. But now, the idea of dismantling internal walls to allow the employee maximum autonomy within the overall company structure is the need. Instead of asking employees, where were they during the working hours, the time has come to ask only, whether the tasks to be performed and the goals to be achieved have been fully accomplished. Take any issue for instance, even today most of our institutes teach classical wage theories without touching the present compensation management practises.

Development Orientation

A ten year old machine cannot be gainfully operated for today's applications with any amount of repairs and modifications. But it is not the case with HR. The more we work, the more we learn leading to better performance and potential enhancement. HRM courses must therefore, be looked into from the holistic developmental perspective with a missionary zeal. The very assumption that HR is a routine maintenance function, needs to be changed as essential developmental function needing delicate professional touch. This change of corporate attitude has to come not by propaganda but by the enduring benefits the human resource development function can bring to the organization.

Viability and Value Addition

There is thinking in the minds of some companies to do away with the HR specialists. They are of the view that HR professionals are mere dogmatic persons, who do not understand the issues and problems of day to day operations in the business. While familiarizing HR professionals to the basics of business operations should be taken care of in the post employment learning immediately after the appointment to the post, there are other subjects like HRM research, proper applications of which can significantly enhance the role and relevance of HR professionals in business. Research is an important area which can help generate basic data to understand the complex issues of HR in business and to devise suitable solutions. For example, one can analyse the failure of mergers and acquisitions of companies which took place without considering the human element involved in this process. Proper research data on HR would not only help taking successful decisions but also enhance the essence and credibility of HR professionals. Therefore teaching of subjects like research methods in HR education requires greater impetus.

Mere theoretical inputs, are in no way going to enhance the self-esteem and confidence of the students to take up managerial jobs immediately after the course. It has got to be practical, for example, the HRM students must know how to conduct interviews, how to devise a performance appraisal system or how to negotiate pay fixation with a talented employee. It is time the colleges identify organizations who can take the responsibility to provide meaningful on the job learning opportunities to the students right from the beginning of the course and at least ¼th of the course duration is devoted to on the job learning.

Today information is transmitted at the speed of light just by click of a button. In this fast changing environment of technology revolution, HRM education cannot be taught with reference to manual typewriters and village postman. The best of information technology courses suitable for HRM must be taught. This measure will make the HRM work process easier, improve efficiency and help the HR professionals to become techno-savvy change agents for the better.

Learning Tools and Methods

Some of the management institutions are still using the blackboard- chalk methods of teaching. Libraries are added more and more with readymade text books in paper form. While the value of blackboard or books in paper form cannot be underestimated at any point of time, there is need to bear in mind their limitations for accelerated learning. Now there are better alternatives, like slide projectors, video films, compact disks and other multimedia tools for enhanced learning. Books in electronic form, video conferencing, internet facilities, and library networks are some of the other learning mediums. There are also audio cassettes for learning so as to reduce strain on the eyes. The institutions must therefore consider using the best of available tools for value added learning.

There has been a debate about the ratio of theory classes to field work and on the job learning during the course of study. The social work courses use the four days theory : two days fieldwork per week pattern. Apart from this, there is also six weeks summer placement and orientation visits. Business management students go for 6-8 weeks summer placements. But rest of those who enter HR profession don't have fieldwork exposure unless they are already employed. It is therefore essential for all HRM education institutions to give adequate importance to the value added learning methods like, fieldwork, on the job learning, case studies, group discussions, role plays, business games, paper presentations, simulation exercises etc. Different methods of learning also reduces the monotony and boredom of blackboard method.

The Role of Teachers

The most important person who has to play predominant role in adding value to the Human Resource Management education is the teacher. A teacher has to be a total person, who can read the books and other reference materials and understand them properly, be able to effectively communicate the lessons with the students by speaking, writing and reading, be able to detect the mistakes of the students and help them to correct, be able to learn continuously, generate knowledge and pass on the new knowledge to the students, be a socially honest person who does not discriminate against any student based on social origins, be an intellectually honest person who doesn't teach wrongly due to his mental prejudice and be a role model to the students who is disciplined, hard working, intelligent, helping, dependable, honest, empathetic, inclined to receive feedback even from students, doesn't take revenge, doesn't indulge in politics, free from bad habits and capable of correcting his mistakes with an open mind.

INDIVIDUAL INITIATIVES

Any movement, any idea or any achievement have never been a reality without the initiatives of individuals involved in the process. Same is the case with HRM education. The individuals namely the students have to work hard to learn better. They must consider enrolling for additional courses through correspondence or open university streams, so as to sharpen their employable skills and narrow down the gap between classroom learning and workplace demands of the competencies. They being the students of post graduate level are expected to involve themselves in basic studies like going through the professional journals, taking up case studies and finding out solutions to live problems. There are a number of professional associations like the National Institute of Personnel Management, National HRD network and Indian society for Training and Development, who conduct seminars, workshops, evening lectures etc. and attending to them can provide not only interactive learning opportunities but help in networking among students, teachers and the industry managers.

ACADEMIC ENVIRONMENT

Some universities do not provide conducive academic environment for qualitative learning of HRM. Lack of sufficient number of competent teachers, non-availability of relevant books and journals, politicizing the academic issues etc. are some of the contemporary problems for learning. As a result the students are compelled by circumstances to look for readymade notes to write their examinations. Real learning and application of creative ideas take a back seat. Reforming the university system will take a longer time, but opening more number of autonomous institutions of learning will help to improve the situation.

THE COST OF EDUCATION

Qualitative management education must be made available at affordable price, failing which it will be monopolized by the elite few. Mounting cost of good education will encourage the students to indulge in unethical practices on the job, so as to recover the huge money spent on education. The economically weaker sections would be virtually deprived of qualitative management education. Therefore it has to be priced in such a way which is affordable to majority population. Need based financial support may also be extended to all the deserving students from economically weaker sections of the society.

THE ETHICS OF ENTRY PROCEDURE

The admission procedures relating to management education requires careful re-examination. For example, majority of the students in India do their graduation courses in the local language. But management education entrance tests are administered in English, thereby keeping away majority students community from entering this important field of education. It is therefore necessary to consider other alternatives like administering the entrance test in the local language, which majority of the students are familiar with. After the admission the English deficient students may be taught a special course on learning English language.

POST EMPLOYMENT HRM EDUCATION

If there is any area in HRM education which has received enormous attention and improvement in the process of liberalization and globalization, it is the post employment education. The new rules of business has brought tremendous pressures on HR departments to ensure retention, training, motivation and result orientation of the talented employees. In fact, many pre-employment HR educational institutions have not improved their learning facilities to the extent and speed required by the modern organizations. But the employers are taking this initiative to get the best out of their talented employees. The individual employees are also sharpening their existing skills and acquiring new skills on their own so as to avoid becoming obsolete in the corporate labour market. In the new economic order employees are required to perform as per global standards and therefore the facilities of learning are also of the same standard. The concept of learning has acquired foremost importance, in fact better learning opportunities in an organization has become, one of the important factors for talented professionals to decide whether to join it or not. The best of inhouse learning facilities have emerged in the form of corporate universities. Added to that the information technology revolution has helped many companies to initiate online learning for their employees around the clock. Reputed universities have introduced the novel courses like executive MBAs and executive Doctorates. Many organizations have come forward to reimburse as much as upto 50,000 rupees per year per employee for acquiring and sharpening the required skills. Education through informal groups, eastern learning philosophy and deputation to overseas learning facilities have become common.

CONCLUSION

In all the important professions like medicine, accountancy, law etc. the professionals are educated in such a way to be able to find solutions themselves. They rarely seek the assistance of others and if at all it is required then they consult only the seniors in their own profession. But unfortunately the education in HRM has been so generalized, that they cannot handle even simple issues on their own. To deduct the income tax of the employees, tax consultant has to assist, to design a performance evaluation form an HRD expert is required and to counsel an employee a counsellor will be hired. Therefore HRM education must be designed in such a way so as to prepare students as total professionals of competency. This will also help the organizations to recognize HRM as an essential profession for realizing the business goals.

▶HR and OD Interventions for Enhancing Organizational Effectiveness◀

CHAPTER

5

infosys campus finishing school:

an empirical case of a HR initiative to gain competitive people advantage in Infosys Technologies Ltd.

SUDAKSHINA GHOSH AND DIPTI

* Sudakshina Ghosh and Dipti_Zachariah are with the Learning and Development Group - HRD, Infosys Technologies Ltd.

Today, business is seeing transformation at a speed never before. To survive and grow in this dynamic business environment, the 'people advantage' can be the only sustainable 'competitive advantage that organizations today can build. In 'Competitive Advantage through People' (Pfeffer, J, 1996)[1], the author rejects Michael Porter's acclaimed positions on the overriding significance of competitors, market substitutes, buyers and suppliers. Pfeffer (1996) says that managers cannot rely solely "on technology, patents, or strategic position" because "Product life cycles are shortening and new-product introductions are coming much more rapidly". He stipulates instead that "people and how we manage them are becoming more important."

Thereby, Pfeffer shows that organizations that support, encourage, and build the skills of their people outperform all competitors. Expanding on this thesis, he discusses creating detailed procedures for employee training, development and participation in the corporation's life and how the above is becoming more and more critical for the sustenance and growth of organizations today.

Keeping the above proposition in mind, Infosys Technologies Ltd strove to build 'people advantage'[1], as a strategic business advantage at all levels. In order to however, achieve the same, we, at Infosys have redefined ways of looking at many traditional concepts of HR to suit the changing needs of business. The following case that we are going to present is one such HR initiative which contributes to building the skills of the people to outperform competitors by bringing about a paradigm shift in the process of employee training & development at the entry level in the organization. Further, this intervention also embraces the latest methodologies to ensure effectiveness of training and provides many solutions to some of the typical challenges faced in the field of training.

THE BUSINESS NEED

Quality of people is the key - nothing can be more true than this— for Infosys operating in a knowledge-based environment, present in a highly competitive industry with ever-rising customer expectations, facing an increasing demand for skilled-manpower and driven by a vision of 'We will be a globally respected

1. Vol. No 1., Pfeffer, Jeffrey, *Competitive Advantage through People: Unleashing the Power of the Work Force*, (edition number 1996).

corporation that provides best-of-breed business solutions, leveraging technology, delivered by best-in-class people". Although, Infosys recruits some of the country's best talents, by following a policy of recruiting the best of the talent from the best of the institutes, a gap was felt between the Infosys desired levels of personal excellence versus the actual standard of people that we recruited, at entry level.

Studies assigned the reason for this gap to the fact that the graduates out of the most prestigious institutes were technically competent, however, the curriculum did not provide them adequate opportunity to develop personal excellence to the Infosys desired levels. This became even more critical as the nature of business in this industry and the increasingly expanding business needs prompted freshers to get into extensive client interfacing roles at the earliest. The organization has always believed in leveraging on each and every client interaction, by converting every 'moment of truth' with the client into a 'golden' or a 'memorable' experience. Given these conditions and with the increasingly tough challenge from the business, the HR in Infosys felt a need for a developmental training, coaching and assessment programme for all entry level joinees, to speed them up to the desired business standards.

Campus Finishing School: An HR Strategic Initiative for 'People Advantage'

The **"Campus Finishing School"** launched in the year 2000 is a response to these critical business needs and is aimed towards–

- Facilitating the development of the required competencies of personal excellence for the role profile of a software engineer at entry level.
- Improving the internal efficiency of functioning within projects by ensuring that less time and energy is spent in coaching the new joinees while on the job.
- Reducing the turn around time of entry-level joinees to that of competent software professionals.
- Providing a competitive advantage to the organization through the quality of people servicing the clients.

- Partnering with the Recruitment Group to meet the business needs of ensuring increased customer satisfaction.

Campus Finishing School: The Methodology

To translate the business requirement into a developmental curriculum, we recognized the need to involve all stakeholders in this process as an integral part of design. The two main methodologies employed were:

- *Focus group discussions* with the fresh recruits to understand their perspective on the nature of skills that are critical and the methodology through which they could assimilate and implement the learning in a continuous manner.
- *Feedback* from business units, especially project managers on their experience and expectations from fresh recruits in their team.

This led to the design of a 10 day managerial training and coaching – programme for all new joinees and was seamlessly integrated with the existing 3.5 months of technical training. The Campus Finishing School as a package addresses several

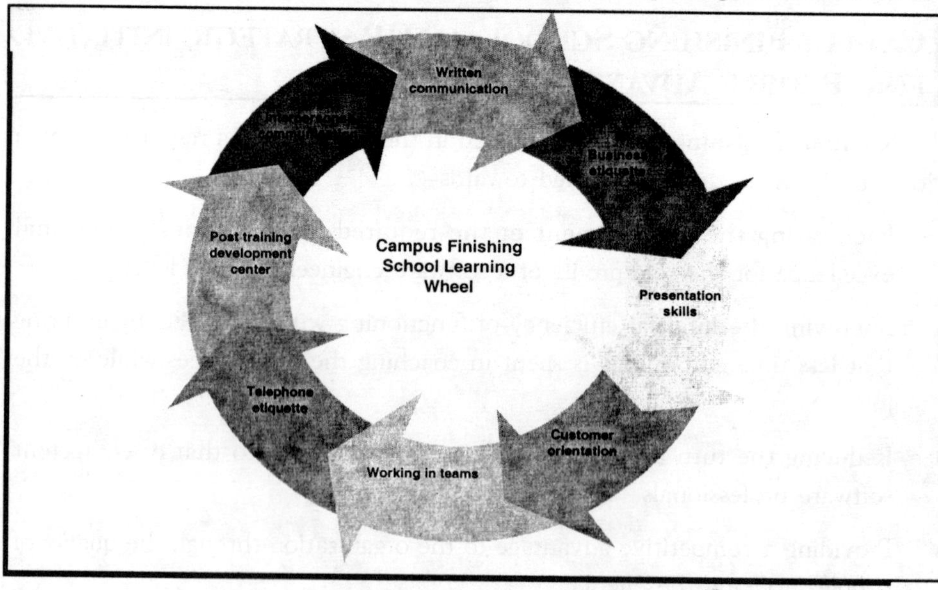

Figure 1

areas of competencies that are required to perform effectively at the entry level. The following model illustrates all the areas that are covered in the form of various learning sessions.

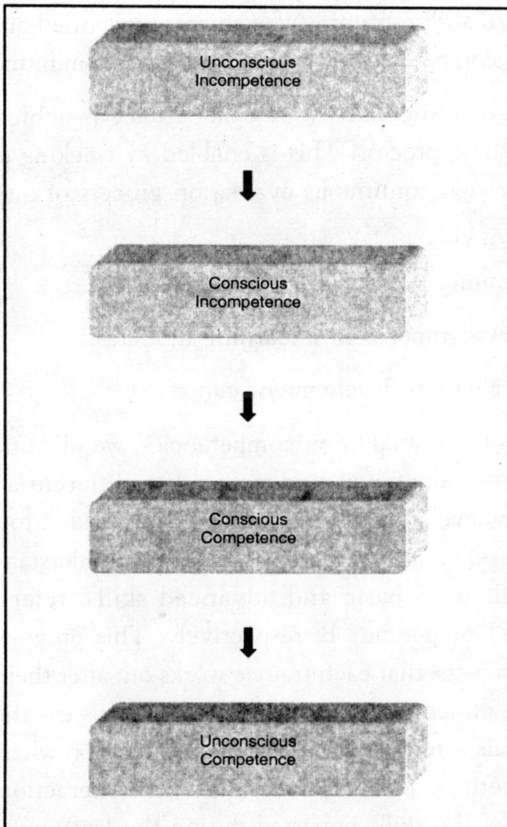

Figure 2

To ensure the effectiveness of the Campus Finishing curriculum, the theory of the four stages of learning by Abraham Maslow*[2] was adopted. This was to facilitate the internalization of managerial and behavioural skills in the trainees in a sequential manner.

We believe that when trainees join this program they are at Stage One of Unconscious Incompetence. The Stage Two of Conscious Incompetence is achieved

2. Calabrese Prudence, *When The Training Stops, The Learning Begins* at http://www.hrvg2.org/newsletter/2001-05/learning.html

through classroom learning sessions or the e-learning sessions in order to develop the various competencies as described in the Campus Finishing School Learning Wheel. In these sessions, the awareness of knowledge and skills related to the competencies is aimed at. Pre-training assessments are carried out to enable trainees to realize their own competency gaps to ensure their commitment to learning.

The Stage three of creating Conscious Competence is achieved by continuous evaluation and coaching process. This is enabled by tracking effectiveness of the learning sessions through continuous evaluation process of measuring knowledge gain using:

- Pre and post training assessments for each module.
- Cases/Quizzes/Assignments in e-learning modules.
- Post-project evaluation development centre.

At this level, based on our studies on competencies, we identified communication skills as the critical competency that acts a key differentiating factor in the performance at entry level. Thus, going forward we decided to focus and develop the communication skills of the trainees. For better understanding, we classified communication skills into basic and advanced skills, referred henceforth as Competency A and Competency B, respectively. This programme also uses the platform of 'mock projects' that each trainee works on, after their technical training to simulate real life project situations, to coach and assess them on managerial skills in the same. This is termed as post project evaluation wherein forums of real-life projects like meetings, presentations, customer interactions and e-mails are used for evaluation of the skills imparted during the learning sessions. A critical ingredient of this phase is continuous feedback for development. Different rounds of audit of skills are conducted to ensure improvement. Special one-to-one feedback and coaching is also provided to trainees to facilitate greater learning. Senior resources from the delivery are trained to evaluate these trainees on standardized parameters and provide feedback. This is to ensure that the trainees meet the actual work-scenario standards. Thus, the post project evaluation acts as a development centre for the trainees.

The Stage four of Unconscious Competence is the level when individuals internalize these skills and behaviour. This is facilitated by using the following process. Once these trainees are released to the business units, they are given the opportunity to experience the real on-the-job scenarios and to implement their learnings there. After 3 months of their release into the projects, they are once again brought back to the programme wherein, a set of assessments are conducted by certified panelists of senior resources from the delivery, on standardized parameters. This is to ensure that the trainees, once given opportunities to try out their learnings in real life scenarios have actually internalized the learnings and are at par with the Infosys desired levels of the quality of people.

RESULTS ACHIEVED

Campus Finishing School, thus has enabled us to recruit the best technically competent candidates from institutes and to develop them in the critical personal excellence skills at the desired levels in-house. By integrating continuous assessments in the system, we have been able to tangibly measure the improvements to form a business case to justify the return on investment. An analysis for one new-joinee batch of last year as they traveled the path of unconscious incompetence to unconscious competencies presented as follows.

When the trainees join the Campus Finishing School process, they are at the level of unconscious incompetence or Stage 2. Thus, during the learning sessions, we focus mainly at the knowledge & some amount of skill level of development of all the competency areas as described in the Campus Finishing School Learning Wheel. This improvement is measured through pre & post training assessments as already mentioned, which measures the 'knowledge gain' from the sessions. Here, the knowledge gain ranged from as high as 97% to 34% depending on the complexity of the competency area addressed.

The stage 3 starts on the assumption that the trainees already have the requisite knowledge and creates a forum for practise, coaching & feedback. At this level, as already mentioned, we have focused on the development of Competencies A and B. The focus in stage 3 is like that of a Development Centre. Continuous feedback is given for improvement by a panel of certified trained resources from the organization on the three round of 'audits' on the imparted skills are conducted in simulated situations. A sample of the positive changes & development of the competencies as demonstrated in simulations is reflected in the examples below:

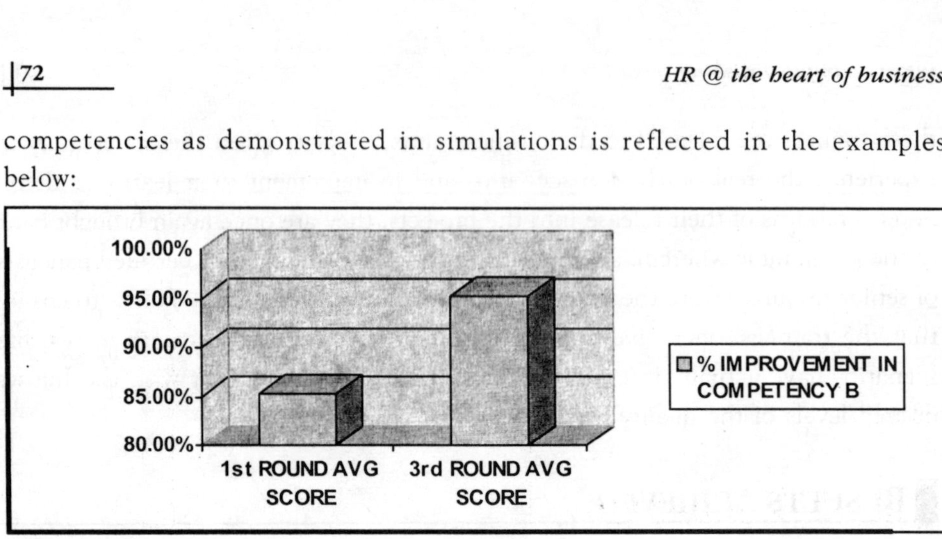

Figure 3

The assumptions for the Stage 4 is that the trainees have got forums of practise in simulated situations and have acquired a certain level of competency in each of the areas. These trainees are then allowed to experience real-life work situations and coached to internalize the learnings from the interventions. After a period of approximate 3-4 months, these trainees are brought into another simulated setting of assessment. This is to check for the actual level of internalization of the learnings & desired behaviour. A panel of trained & certified resources on predefined parameters conducts assessments to assess the internalization of Competency A and B through demonstrated behaviours. The following are the results of a comparative analysis between the Stage 3 absolute results & the Stage 4 results,

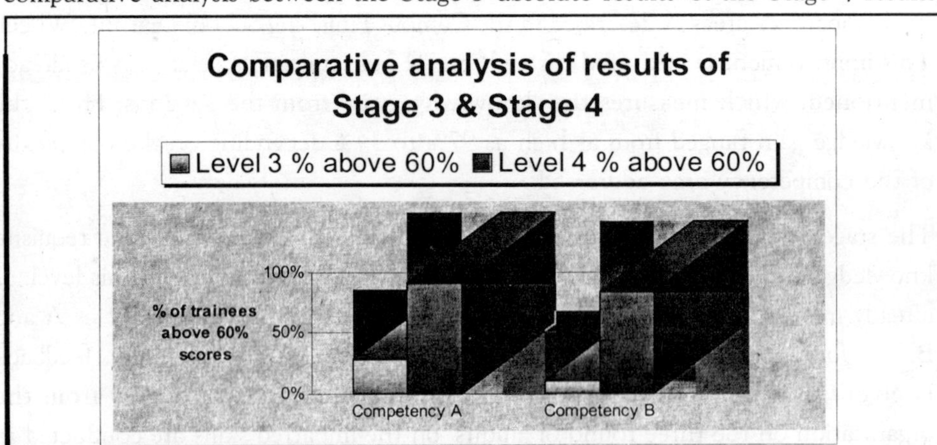

Figure 4

which confirms our assumption that trained behaviour once with real-life exposure results in greater internalization of the competencies.

Thus, by using Maslow's model of Four Stages of Learning, we have been able to train the entry level on broadly all the competencies required at the level, while extensively coaching and monitoring the development of the critical ones.

THE BUSINESS BENEFITS

The business benefits from such an initiative can be seen both in the partnering with other groups in HR like recruitment and also by the business value addition which is reflected in the customer satisfaction, both internal as well as external.

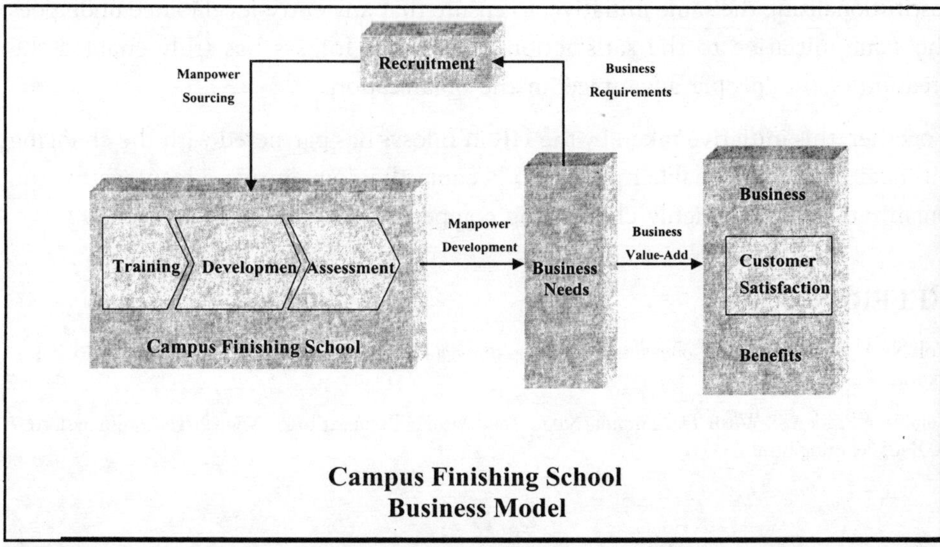

Figure 5

Improved customer service and satisfaction has thus emerged as the ultimate benefit from this initiative. This is highlighted by the positive feedback from our project managers and business managers as experienced by them in course of the projects, as one of the senior project manager says, "I feel this Campus Finishing School is an excellent initiative as it has demonstrated tangible results. For instance, me and my colleagues feel that the quality of people joining today at entry level is much better that what we had in the same level earlier."

By partnering with the Infosys vision of providing the best in class business solutions, we have tangibly improved the customer service. Today, we have more and more competent people handling client transactions right from the time they join the projects fresh from campuses.

Redefining Training for a strategic intervention for developing 'People advantage'

What this initiative has done in the field of HR in organizations is that it has exploded the concepts of traditional classroom training and has defined newer horizons. Campus Finishing School moves away from traditional notions of training by embracing a 'trainee need centric' intervention, which integrates different training, development and assessment mechanisms to result in tangible behaviour change. This initiative in itself also answers many of the typical questions of the actual training effectiveness and the return on investment in training. By institutionalizing the same initiative, to ensure that any entry-level joinee undergoes the same initiative to the satisfaction, the HR in Infosys has truly enabled the creation of the 'people advantage' in the organization.

Together, this initiative taken by the HR in Infosys has partnered with the changing business needs and enabled people to become the competitive advantage for the organization in this highly challenging competitive environment.

REFERENCES

Vol. No 1., Pfeffer, Jeffrey, *Competitive Advantage through People: Unleashing the Power of the Work Force*, (edition number 1996).

Calabrese Prudence, *When The Training Stops, The Learning Begins* at http://www.hrvg2.org/newsletter/2001-05/learning.html

CHAPTER

6

appreciative inquiry (AI) for building learning organizations

V M RAMALINGAM*

* V M Ramalingam, a postgraduate from Madras University (1964), has over 36 years of experience in organizations. He is a freelance consultant and a member of Group for Institution Development, Bangalore.

All problems are created in the human mind. We look at problems to solve rather than the potential to overcome them. In the book, "Leaders" by Warren Bennis and Burt Nanus, I read about "Walenda Factor". Carl Walenda was the most successful aerialist of the century. He fell to his death at Rio-de-Janeiro when he, for the first time, focused on not falling. The plants grow by moving in the direction of sunlight. But as human beings, are we looking at our 'heliotropic' tendency to grow ? We survive and grow because we know what gives us "light" is within us and take effort in that direction.

The human cultures and civilizations have been evolved by focusing on people's positive energy and strength. These 'life excelling energies' that were experienced by the creators of exceptional moments and landmarks were replicated innovatively in human efforts with improved vigour. Thus, human organizations developed. The human civilizations and institutions of culture developed through the sharing of stories, songs and folklores of valour, successes and achievement of people. The mythologies and epics in every culture are standing examples. The focus was not on problems but on the way they were overcome through human power. The leaders and the people dreamt a desired future and collectively created the realities of those dreams by using their positive energy. As I see, appreciative inquiry is founded on these thoughts.

About Appreciative Inquiry

Everyone had exceptional, satisfying moments in the past and created landmarks in the journey of life. Appreciative inquiry ("AI") focuses on generating and applying knowledge that comes from inquiry into moments of excellence, periods of exceptional competence and performance. These were times when people have felt most alive and energized. Perhaps, the moments were ecstatic, joyous or euphoric. Also, the moments might have been painful encounters or seen as painful but were moments of achievement. These were enriching, energizing, strengthening, stimulating and satisfying moments. From these moments, we identify our **'life giving forces'** of sustaining and building ourselves. The word "appreciation" also means "value addition".

"AI" can be used as a Total Large System Interactive Process for even 1000 people. It can also be applied for improvement/effectiveness of micro-system (a team, a department, a zone, a division or a unit). It may be a whole system or a microcosm.

"AI" is both a process and a philosophy. It is a process for engaging people in building the kinds of families, communities, organizations and the world, they want to live in. The process in totality comprises of five phases: Definition, Discovery, Dream, Design, and Delivery/Destiny.

As an OD intervention - complex system change, all the five phases can be facilitated. Otherwise, as methodology, the middle three phases can be adapted as part of any other programme. The AI can be integrated with other methodologies suitably. But the basic tenets will remain the same. I have personally experienced appreciative inquiry to be quite effective in my professional work.

HISTORY OF APPRECIATIVE INQUIRY

The history of Appreciative Inquiry is the history of a major shift in the practise of organization development and transformation. As a young doctoral student David Cooperrider started his research under his guide Suresh Srivastva of Case Western Reserve University, Cleveland in the year 1980. The outcome of the research is Appreciative Inquiry. It was initiated not as an approach to organizational change but as a social theory-building process. In 1987, David Cooperrider and Suresh Srivatsava published the article, "Appreciative Inquiry in Organizational Life". The impact of this publication on practitioners in the field of applied behavioural science has been significantly path breaking. There has been a paradigm shift in the approach towards Action Research, OD and HRD for facilitating change in human systems. The genesis of the theory culminated as a practise for organizational change and in 1994 professional development workshop in Appreciative Inquiry was offered for the first time by NTL Institute of Applied Behavioural Science, USA.

Richard Beckhard, one of the founders of Organization Development (OD) had this to say in the symposium of the "Past, Present, and Future of Organization Development", organized by National Academy of Management, USA, in August 1999:

"Appreciative Inquiry is, in my view, an exciting breakthrough, one that signals a change in the way we think about change. I'm intrigued by how rapidly it is emerging; but it is something substantive, conceptually strong, not like the quick fads. In my view, we are looking at something important - AI will be of enduring consequence and energizing innovation for the field of OD. That's my prediction."

In 1996, "The Organization Development Practitioner" published an issue completely devoted to "AI", and in 2000, it devoted its millennium special issue to "AI". The editor, Peter Sorenson argued that "AI" is more than a method; it is a paradigm change uniquely created for the opportunities of the 21st century.

"AI" AS A PHILOSOPHY OF CHANGE AND A WAY OF BEING IN THE WORLD

Appreciative Inquiry as a philosophy:

- emphasises collaboration and participation of all voices in the system or sub-system - generates inclusion processes - enlarges and compounds energy.
- approaches change as a journey (rather than an event) - continuously happening in the organization, not at any one time (learning organization)
- has a system orientation (focus is on changing the organization/system rather than the people)
- values continuity along with innovation and transition management; (in every human system, there is something worth preserving and build on)
- most uniquely, builds on the "life giving forces" present when a system is performing optimally in human, economic and organizational terms (spirituality of the system as a human collective).

Appreciative Inquiry is grounded in social constructionist thought, a worldview that asserts that we use "language" to create the world as we know and understand it. Words create the world. If positive beliefs, abundant hopes and awareness of strengths are shared among people, the world grows and flourishes. On the other hand, if fears, negative thoughts, deficiencies and the ways of correcting them float in the language of sharing or folklores, stagnation and degeneration set in.

Recently, in my programme on Appreciative Inquiry, a participant stated as follows: "Improvement means avoiding and correcting deficiencies of a person or system. Without focusing on problems and solving them, we cannot grow or become effective. So I am not impressed by AI as it ignores the defects and mistakes."

I responded that "AI" is not just praising people and it does not ignore problems. There is a part in the process of appreciative presentations by the groups when other participants are asked to share their wish-statements. The participants may express the difficulties and problems that currently exist. After all, this kind of experience of pain and struggle often propels the drive to change. "AI" practitioners don't advocate denying negative emotions or problems. However, they encourage participants not to dwell on them. Focus is not on solving the problems but building the prosperous future. In the process, the problems get dissolved. The belief is that improvement means increasing the strength and using it more frequently. Absence of sickness is not health. But a healthy person does not fall sick often.

At the end of the programme, after going through simulations of AI phases, the participant informed that the experiences in the programme generated useful insights about the possibilities, and above all, he told that he had learnt to appreciate himself.

Carl G Jung, a great psychologist says,

"All the greatest and most important problems of life are fundamentally insoluble... They can never be solved, but only outgrown with a new and stronger life urge."

The five core processes of Appreciative Inquiry are:

1. Choose the positive as the focus of inquiry.
2. Inquire into stories of life giving forces.

3. Locate themes that appear in the stories.
4. Create shared images of a preferred future.
5. Innovate ways to create that future.

"AI involves, in a central way, the art and practise of asking questions that strengthen a system's capacity to apprehend, anticipate and heighten positive potential. It centrally involves the mobilization of inquiry through the crafting of the "unconditional positive question" often involving hundreds and sometimes, thousands of people. In AI, the arduous task of intervention gives way to the speed of imagination and innovation. Instead of negation, criticism, and spiraling diagnosis, there is discovery, dream and design. AI fundamentally seeks to build a constructive union between a whole people and the massive entirety of what people talk about as past and present capacities: achievements, assets, unexplored potentials, innovations, strengths, elevated thoughts, opportunities, benchmarks, high point moments, lived values, traditions, strategic competencies, stories, expressions of wisdom, insights into the deeper corporate spirit or soul and visions of valued and possible futures." David Cooperrider **(co-originator of "AI")**

The 5-D model - the practical change process of AI

This model has been developed by Jane Watkins and Bernard Mohr as an improvement over the original 4-D model used in GEM initiative of USAID.

1. ***A Definition*** phase during which the goals, including the framing of the question and the inquiry protocol, the participation strategy, and the project management structure are developed.
2. A ***Discovery*** phase during which members from the system develop an in-depth understanding of (a) the life-giving properties that are present in those exceptional moments when the organization is performing optimally in human, economic, and organizational terms, and (b) the structures, dynamics, and other associated conditions that allow those life-giving properties to flourish.
3. A ***Dream*** phase during which system members create shared images of what their organization would look, be, feel, and function like if those exceptional

moments and the life-giving properties in the system became the norm rather than the exception. This phase guides people towards drawing collectively their "macro provocative propositions".

4. A ***Design*** phase during which system members agree on the principles that should guide changes in the organization's socio-technical architecture and develop the details of whatever changes are thought to be needed, based on the previously articulated guiding principles. In this phase, people draw their micro provocative propositions which may be based on either the individual action approach or the whole system (may be a sub-system) design approach.
5. A ***Destiny*** phase sometimes called the ***Delivery*** phase, during which the organization evolves into the preferred future image created during the dream phase using the work done in the design phase. It is the phase of implementation of the action-plans drawn on the basis of micro provocative propositions and institutionalizing the AI processes. The destination is that the organization becomes a learning organization.

EXPERIENCES IN AI

There is no one right way to engage in Appreciative Inquiry and the process can take different forms. The variations may be on the topic of inquiry, the process for discovering exceptional moments, the method used in dreaming new futures, and the innovations developed in the design and delivery phases. I cite some examples of application of AI from my professional practise.

Episode-1

We responded to a call from a manufacturing company to design and conduct a programme for union leaders. It is an annual feature in the company but this year's programme had special significance as the mood of employees and the management was sad and disturbed due to impact from the market, and cost cutting.

The attitude of the management and HR executives was proactive and empathetic towards employees. The dilemma in their minds was about balancing the organizational interest with employee welfare.

The two-day programme facilitated by myself and my colleague Raja Chidambaram applying "AI" processes started off with an open and plain keynote presentation about the organization's current challenges by a very senior executive of the company. The discovery phase progressed through identifying the 'life giving forces'. Between discovery and dreaming Phase, there were turmoils and struggles. Ultimately, the group realized the importance of looking at positive possibilities. The outcome of the participants' mood was tempered in positive outlook about the organizational interest. After the programme was over, there was an interface of the union leaders with the senior executives of the company. The process of deliberations was reported to be smooth and meaningful. The programme was useful in diluting the blaming mood and redirecting their thoughts from the tendency of digging into what has gone wrong in the past. The focus shifted to the future possibilities.

Episode-2

The experience with the 'Society for Promotion of Wasteland Development (SPWD)' was different. Swiss Development Agency (SDA) invited me in January 2002 to work with their project coordinators (the internal consultants) who were on an assignment of evaluation for strengthening SPWD. Dr. Anuradha Prasad and Dr. Patrick Robinson, the internal consultants identified "AI" as the appropriate methodology at that stage of their evaluation studies. The SPWD was founded in early eighties by Dr.M.S.Swaminathan and his colleague-scientists. Over a period of two decades, the society implemented many projects funded by SDA and other agencies. In 2001, there was a felt need to increase the effectiveness and expansiveness of project implementation by the society. The SDA took the initiative through the evaluation study. After a few diagnostic interventions, the internal consultants involved me in the work on 'AI'. During the inauguration of the programme, the acting Chairman announced that the Executive Director, the CEO of the SPWD has resigned as he was being hospitalized for heart ailment .The Chairman's position also was vacant. The acting Chairman and a Director, both of them scientists, were present during the programme. In the 2-day programme at Delhi, the 18 participants worked for more than 20 hours (net) with full of energy inspite of receiving the initial shock about the CEO's exit. The participants were regional coordinators heading the operations of the society in different regions spread throughout India.

The group prepared participatively the macro and micro provocative propositions for realizing their collective dream – the desired future state for SPWD. They carried their convictions and action-plans as the output of the workshop. The workshop was acclaimed by the target group and the internal consultants of the SDC as an energizing intervention. The documentation of the process and outcome of the intervention was useful in preparing the report of the consultants.

Episode-3

The General Manager in charge of operations suddenly expired creating a leadership vacuum. The managers of departments wanted to explore the possibilities of 'collective leadership' to face the formidable challenges emerging from internal and external realities. After a sensing meeting, based on their diagnosis, my colleagues Raja Chidambaram and Halasyam invited me to join in for the designing and conducting the programme. We designed and conducted an AI based workshop for two days. It was an exciting experience for us since the group of managers empowered themselves to draw an action plan to achieve certain specified goals with a time frame ending on 31st March 2003. The participants informed that the programme was really helpful to reinforce their hope and vigour.

In all these programmes, 'moderation method' was used for capturing data, visualization, presentation and documentation.

Creating a Learning Organization

Appreciative Inquiry enables organizations to build their own generative theory for enabling transformational shifts by learning from their most positively exceptional moments. Thus, the organizations evolve themselves as learning organizations building on the appreciative learning culture. By going through the five phases continually, the culture accentuates *the successes of the past, evokes images of possible futures, and creates an ongoing inquiry* that empowers members to new levels of activity. The appreciative learning cultures develop specific competencies:

1. ***Affirmative Competence.*** The organization draws on the human capacity to appreciate positive possibilities by selectively focusing on current and past strengths, successes, and potentials.
2. ***Expansive Competence.*** The organization challenges habits and conventional practises, provoking members to experiment in the margins, makes expansive promises that challenge them to stretch in new directions, and evokes a set of higher values and ideals that inspire them to passionate engagement.
3. ***Generative Competence.*** The organization constructs integrative systems that allow members to see the consequences of their actions, to recognize that they are making a meaningful contribution, and to experience a sense of newness through progress.
4. ***Collaborative Competence.*** The organization creates forums in which members engage in an ongoing dialogue and exchange diverse perspectives.

The key to sustaining the learning in organizations is to build systems, procedures and practises with an appreciative approach. The approach is non-threatening and energizing people. "AI" is of new paradigm. Each time you work with it will be different. It has the power of being totally unique to any group that takes this route to organization transformation and renewal. This core process is ongoing. It is full of continuing dialogue; revisited and updated discussions and provocative propositions. The process comprises of additional interviewing sessions, especially with new members of the organization. It sustains a high level of innovation and continued learning.

For example, one company accelerates its learning through an annual strategic planning conference that involves all five hundred people in the firm as well as key partners and stakeholders. As a setting for strategic learning, teams present their benchmarking studies of the best 5 other organizations, deemed leaders in their class. Other teams present an annual appreciative analysis of development initiatives and, together these data bases of success stories (internal and external) help set the stage for the company's strategic, future search planning. The entire process culminates in an annual "AI" summit for strategic planning. The enthusiasm flows abundantly in every participant. People reinforce their life giving forces, generate collective focus on organization's purpose with hope of success, and learn to appreciate each other, empower themselves and nurture a sense of belonging among themselves. This system creates a structure to build the company into a learning organization. The five disciplines of a learning organization as conceptualized by Peter Senge are personal mastery, shift in mental models, shared vision, team learning, and systems thinking. All these disciplines are ingrained in Appreciative Inquiry.

NOTE: *The basic tenets and the Five-D model have been sourced from the reading materials prepared by Jane Magruder Watkins and Bernard J.Mohr for the programmes on Appreciative Inquiry conducted by Taos Institute and NTL Institute of Applied Behavioural Science, USA. They are the co-creators of 'AI' and the Facilitators of the Professional Development Programmes on 'AI'.*

CHAPTER

7

mergers & acquisitions : develop a merger competency model

BALAGURU MOHANADOSS*

* Balaguru Mohanadoss heads M/s. HR Net Consultants Pvt. Ltd. - specializing on KM, PCMM, Leadership Development and Culture Building.

Mergers and acquisitions have become a common strategic practise to face global competition. A deeper study reveals that there are different strategic objectives, drivers, problems which can be classified as short, medium and long term drivers that propel the mergers and acquisitions. The complexity becomes more challenging especially when they are across continents and integrate two different cultures.

This paper recommends three-pronged strategy to make mergers a sustainable corporate tool.

Firstly, use a pre-merger Cultural Assessment Tool (CAT) to assess the cultural character of an organization based on discrete characteristics.

Secondly, develop a Merger Competency Model (MCM) that would radically improve the ability of an organization to assess the environment, create structures, develop strategies and formulate policies that would attract, retain and develop leaders; thus retain the merger capability. The business objectives taking into account the drivers in the environment, set the business imperatives that are measurable components formulates the Merger Competency Model. This helps to further work on a Developmental Model and Merger Proficiency Model (basket of competencies).

Finally, in the prognosis, prophesises that organizations require different type of leaders at different levels of the organization and functions, in tune with drivers, objectives and problems faced in a merger. Hence, the need to develop a Merger Proficiency Model (MPM) to have a basket of proficiencies related to performance, relationship, managerial and leadership. These would help to merge, blend cultures, and institutionalize practises that would build a culture of continuous renewal and progress, impacting every facet of human life.

INTRODUCTION

Globalization has thrown open opportunities aplenty amidst increased market competition. Companies have realized the importance of remaining competitive in ensuring survival and growth; have resorted to measures, such as restructuring, alliances, joint ventures, mergers and acquisitions. Mergers and acquisitions have become a common strategic practise and a tool to achieve faster growth and market leadership position.

As Feros, Lewis puts it: "Mergers are People". Hence, HR strategy in any merger or acquisition process has to be an integral part of the business strategy. The business strategy in a pre-merger may be to look for a strategic fit in a partner. But to ensure that the strategic fit delivers results, in post merger, the people support gained through an effective HR strategy is essential.

DRIVERS FOR MERGERS AND ACQUISITION

The twin drivers - globalization and technology, operating simultaneously have ushered in the new Economy into India in more recent times. Organizations have been responding to such changes in the environment by organic growth or by acquiring / merging organizations into their fold.

There are organizations that want to shape the future. They shape the rules of the game rather than being ruled by rules of the game. These companies learn to anticipate the possible directions that the future may take and begin to blaze the new path without hesitation. The leaders of these companies encourage their people to challenge conventional thinking and to create continuous renewal and progress. Renewal challenges the company to stretch and grow. For most of the companies, continuous renewal is more than a catchphrase; it is their culture (Dauphinais). There are irreversible changes in forces that are driving these changes. We could call these the new economic drivers. There are three kinds of drivers with varying amplitude and time horizons, which will dictate the future of economy and the future of business. They are a) Short-term drivers b) Medium-term drivers and c) Long-term drivers.

Short-Term Drivers

These are primarily the various kinds of arbitrage opportunities that exist across various nationalities, economies and regions. The labour cost differential among the software professionals between the US and India was a great arbitrage opportunity on which the initial success of the industry was built – 50 per cent a year compounded for seven years on an increasingly larger base.

Global companies prefer alliances and affiliations with companies in emerging markets, Limitations by Governments, hitherto, limited foreign ownership and this was the only route for global companies to make their presence felt locally. Companies mostly come together with the sole aim of a wider reach or to open new distribution channels. However, the post acquisition phase is marred since alliance partners continue to wear their masks; the problems of running the unit takes major set back and many had failed to meet expectations. Also, most companies lose their revenue momentum while concentrating on cost synergies or failing to focus systematically on post merger growth. Yet in the end, stalled growth hurts a company's market performance far more than a failure to cut costs. In a McKinsey article titled, "Why Mergers fail?" the authors advocate, "Companies that do their best don't rush headlong into attempts to find cost reducing synergies. Rather, those companies first look after existing customers and revenue, retain their revenue generating talent and tailor the integration to balance their revenue and cost initiatives".

The over arching aim would be to do extensive restructuring later on and to redefine the future directions – goals, strategies, financial targets. The proposal is mostly tactical in nature; to strengthen and grow the core business.

Medium-Term Drivers

In this scenario, technological possibilities and changes in the geo-political scenario will be the major economic drivers. These need to be looked into by built-to-last firms for strategic planning. The approach would both be tactical and strategic; broad enough and profound in redirection to the company taking into account:

- Potential impact of new technologies and competitors on company's business;
- Likely strategies of existing competitors;
- New customer and channel requirements;
- Potential market and product strategies;
- Invest in existing and new businesses/markets.

These are the organizations that say, "Beyond Today and Business Operations". The "opportunity based organizational design" allows a company to conduct the day-to-day work of its business units while simultaneously pulling together teams to pursue special opportunities as they arise. McKinsey in its study for these types of organizations have recommended "to balance competing agendas, marshal the resources necessary to serve today's customers while developing tomorrow's". Also suggested to practise:

a) Target the right opportunities

b) Match resources & opportunities

c) Get diverse resources to work together and

d) Develop flexible world-class resources.

The approach is to invest in strategic new products and markets. Companies keep its own research and development efforts sharp by sharing knowledge and innovations with business partners (like Compaq did with partners like Microsoft and Intel) and by investing in early stage technology companies. This provides access to additional expertise in key emerging technologies and product development strategies (Like Compaq's pre-initial public offering investment in Raptor systems, a developer of network security firewalls to meet corporate Internet and Intranet needs).

Long-Term Drivers

Basically fundamental but its impact may not be felt in day-to-day business but they are so pervasive that they impact every facet of human life. This long-term driver represents an unprecedented opportunity for success, growth and wealth creation. Managers and citizens who have collaborated in this effort should use free will and their passion to dream a future and make it happen. Every employee who wants to lead a revolution of their own should take them to heart. This may require collaborative action with the society.

Globalization and WTO's free trade programmes helped manufacturers to invade other countries for revenue growth that consequently lowered their price. The case of GE's lighting division helps to understand this phenomenon. GE was the leading player in North America and was challenged in 1982 by tentative incursions of overseas competitors that became an invasion with companies from Hungary, Poland, Japan, Taiwan and Korea. The new comers offered an unbeatable business proposition; good quality bulbs price below GE's. This price advantage was based in part on labour costs (Tichy).

Why did Philips migrate transatlantic and take over Westinghouse? Philips, the Dutch firm, bought Westinghouse; it fought hard for North American market share and won. Probably, they understood the need for wellspring of profitability, which comes out of revenue growth and productivity. Revenue growth, perhaps the clearest demonstration of customer satisfaction, is essential to maximize profits over the long-term. Productivity is the best measure of efficient operation, as well as a potentially rich source of earnings.

Why did GE lose in its own turf? GE's sales began to drop in 1985 and they had to raise prices to maintain profitability. GE stranded with retail price up to 40% higher than competing brands. It all had happened since the lighting division developed a distinctively complacent corporate culture, relaxed about costs and remarkably willing to pamper employees. The culture of comfort endured, as commented by someone: "The culture was club like – fraternal to the point that relationships counted more than performance".

A new chieftain, abandoning his predecessor's insular approach, defined his Vision and articulated business goals in the context of a world market for lighting products. He charted his thinking down to a few big ideas – "drives". A drive to a) achieve the industry's lowest costs b) increase sales by creating new markets c) lead the world in customer service, with sophisticated fulfillment and distribution systems d) regain leadership in product quality. Once the Vision was formulated and clear, there were two types of Mergers:

First, merged three lighting P & L centres into one - a plant that makes wire, a plant that wraps the wire into coils, and a plant that assembles the coils into lamps. By optimizing each business, one may not optimize the total. But, by organizing three plants as a single unit, they can seek the optimum balance of opportunities. It may make sense to make a costlier wire – if it helps us to produce a cheaper lamp.

In 1989, GE ranked No. 2 in the world market. Yet GE did hardly any business outside North America. In a competition with global players, matching and even beating their prices is not enough. One needs to access competitor's markets, for two reasons: first to maximize one's revenue opportunities; second, to weaken the competitors by attacking them in their home markets, just as Philips had hit GE, earlier.

Secondly, in 1989, GE acquired a majority stake in Tungsram, Hungarian lighting company; also bought light bulb business of Britain's Thorn – thus, GE became a credible opponent to Philips on its own turf.

GE, thus, by its efforts within its group and across border merged units that offered the world's best design and technology at the best price, to community at large. The onerous task before the leader, no doubt, was to change the organizational culture!

WILL CULTURE MAKE THE DIFFERENCE?

Generating a single wave of change is possible but the effects are seldom long-lasting or self-sustaining. When continuous renewal or performance is expected, and if the organizations have not created the right ambience for such an attempt, people become "smart dumps". People have to be willing to accept the risk of change to create a self-sustaining cycle of improvement and an ongoing sense of renewal. That is possible only if employees know that individual and collective success can only continue if they embrace change as an opportunity rather than reacting to it in a crisis mode.

With today's volatility in business, organizations should respond by placing one foot in the present and the other in the future – responding to today's customer needs while preparing for tomorrow's by striving to find the future first. Those who really succeed constantly adapt to the changing environment, managing the dimensions of competition, keeping pace with the design and technology marvels, applying scenario-planning technique, than casually talking about 'aligning parts of the organizations'.

How do we identify the critical and cultural characteristics of organizational longevity, especially, when two different organizations either domestically or across borders marry together? Can we develop an instrument that measures the fit of our Indian organizations that go for alliances and mergers to look into the following factors?

- Critical characteristics that enhance competitiveness of merged organization.
- Influence of culture on executive change decisions.

- Leadership styles that carry through multiple teams with diverged cultural background.
- Process that plug in each other's resources, knowledge and goals.

Cultural Assessment Tool

Kaipa, Prasad says that for any merger or acquisition to be successful, structures, leadership, culture and strategy are going to be critical. You can examine the firm at any level and the DNA remains the same, though functionality and character will change. The culture of a company gives it a character and uniqueness that could be closest to biological DNA. Culture refers to the collection of values, beliefs, behaviours, customers and attitudes that characterize an organization. Each organization has a unique culture and hence, a unique DNA map. Organizational culture consists of stories, symbols, beliefs, and assumptions and values that members have in common. Culture can be inferred from what people say, do, feel and think within in an organizational setting. The culture is largely tacit and is not explicitly defined by rules and structures. It is structurally complex because it consists of large sets of implicit assumptions that cover how employees view their relationships with various environments (customers, suppliers, community, leadership, each other). In other words, the personality of an organization is represented by organizational culture and it influences how people behave within the organizational system. Culture determines, to a large extent, what employees see, hear, and feel and how they respond to each other and the outside world. That is why it is critical for us to understand and map the culture DNA when we look for creating success in a newly merged company. For assessing the cultural character of an organization, the organization could be guided by 14 discrete characteristics viz: governance structure, leadership roles / influence, power, how change is viewed, the basis of planning, the primary mode of problem solving, how control is exerted, communication styles / purpose, marketing focus, performance management, vision/ values, how people are perceived, success definitions and guiding principles/ assumptions.

This would help organizations to assess before making the decision on mergers and acquisitions. Alternatively, this framework would be used to avoid post merger blues and enhance the performance. The tool would also initiate the following steps:

- Create an array of listening posts to sense the future and set the directions for short-term, medium-term and long-term.
- Create and maintain open lines of communication with customers, business partners, industry analysts and other organizations that can provide insight into market and technology trends.
- Guide to build common set of values such as trust and commitment amidst employees to achieve newly evolved business objectives.

When Two Become One - Cultural Integration

How does it feel to put a merger into practise? In a merger, as with marriage, both partners have something that makes the other more complete. The joint venture that combines the existing facilities, people, capital and technology of two very seasoned companies, neither of which can overcome difficult market obstacles alone. People have to be involved in identifying the prevailing norms, values and beliefs in their organizations and work together to incorporate coherent values that would guide the merged entity.

Develop a Merger Competency Model

Companies have yet to learn the lessons from others. Up to three quarters of these deals destroy value that has been the objective of many mergers and acquisitions. Why? Organizations that are high performers and who pursue their transactions as part of a disciplined and ongoing programme, link their transactions to clear strategic goals, and are organized for fast decision making and effective implementation. Most of the companies that have been failing in their M & A efforts have treated M & A, as occasional and major events. In the case of top performers and especially in high tech oriented companies, deal making is an ongoing business process. In an industry that virtually requires companies to do deals, that kind of proficiency is a competitive advantage - detailed as to the timetable of events and major milestones and coherent plans for managing interdependencies.

The change in the environment like globalization, active WTO requires timely responses. A Merger Competency Model that defines the merger leadership characteristics is important for professional success. The motivation is to develop a Merger Competency Model that would radically improve the ability of organizations to assess the environment, create structures, develop strategies and formulate policies that would attract, retain and develop leaders; thus retain the merger capability..

A merger competency model has been arrived at after considering the strategic objective and the key business drivers (Fig 1). The pointers are based on the experiences and the literature review for the components of developmental model, which has to be nurtured by the core team of the merged entity. The components identified are the universally accepted dimensions – Structure, Strategy, People, Process and Leadership.

Structure

Many mergers would not have happened without a consideration of the structure and style of command associated with it. What happens in a decentralized organization vs. in a centralized and hierarchical operation? In a decentralized environment, lots of resources are invested on communication workshops. In a centralized or hierarchical operation, most of the employees spend their whole lives in "command and control" operating style. So, there are two tracks of culture, systems, procedures and protocols. Can there be a fusion – a new corporate culture creation? If there are two strong cultural legacies, they have to be modified and in some cases demolizhed. The goal has to be achieved under severe time pressures and hence a suitable structure that takes into account the values, processes, customer style, image and styles in operation and weld them into an organizational unity. The longer the time taken for unity, the more ground it would lose in the market place. Thus, the fusion process has to be driven by a genuine sense of extreme urgency.

Strategy

Recent merger between IBM and PwC gave Indian PwC partners an opportunity to vote on the merger with IBM; the consulting business of PwC will be merged with the Business Innovation Services Group, which is part of IBM India. (ET 1st Aug). There were other mergers in the past involving Chase, wherein all key managers had a chance to express their points of view. By contrast, the authoritarian,

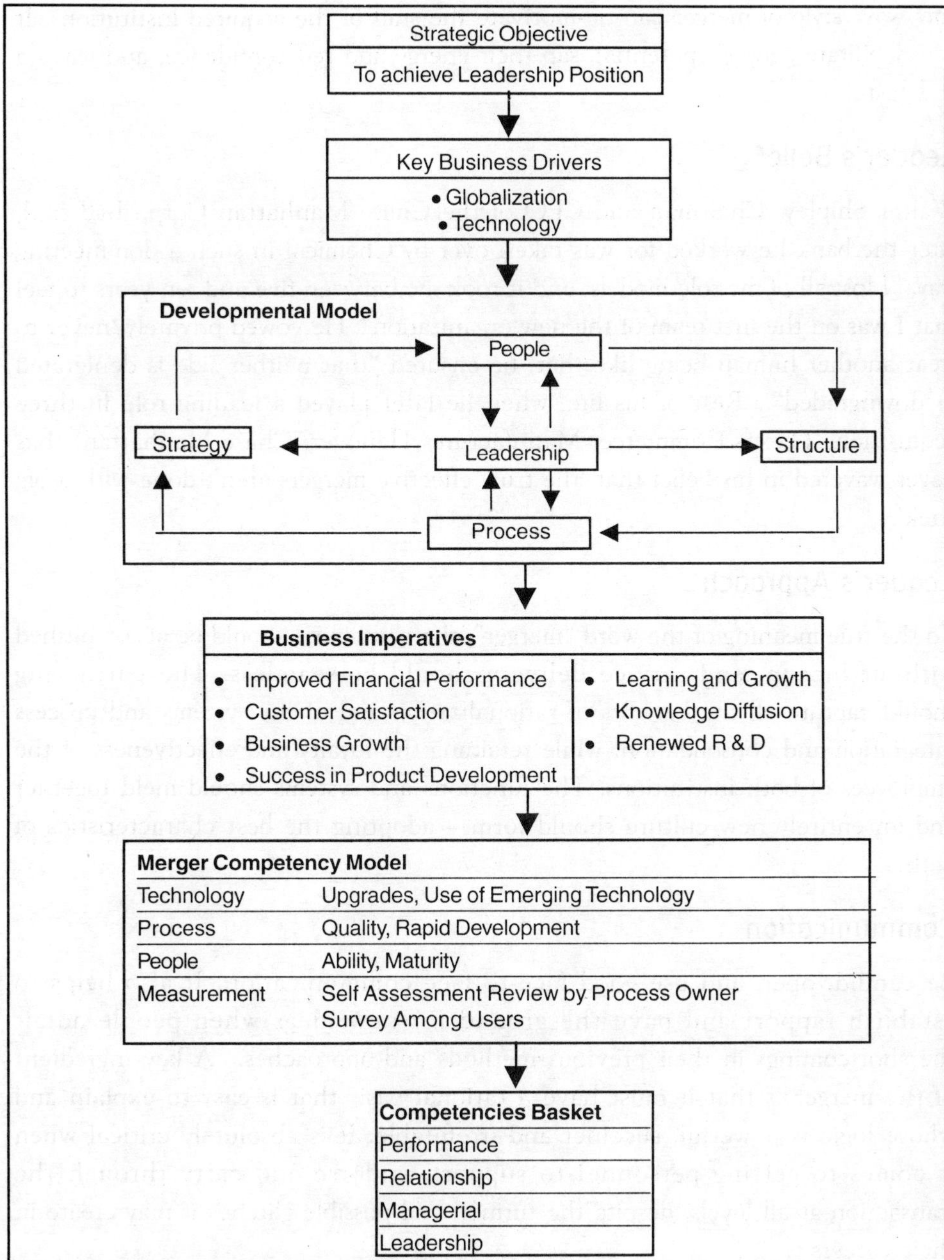

Figure 1 Merger Competency and Developmental Model

"my way" style of merger can de-motivate the staff of the acquired institutions. It can debilitate people's potential, sap their energy and self-confidence, and leave a bad taste.

Leader's Belief

Walter Shipley, Chairman and CEO of the Chase Manhattan Corp., had said, after the bank he worked for was taken over by Chemical in such a domineering way, "I lost all of my role models, and it took me between five and ten years to feel that I was on the first team of the new organization". He vowed privately 'never to treat another human being like that, he ensured "that neither side is denigrated or downgraded". Rest of his life, when he later played a leading role in three acquisitions (Texas Commerce, Manufactures Hanover, Chase Manhattan), has never wavered in his belief that 'the truly effective mergers aren't done with a big stick'.

Leader's Approach

To the true meaning of the word "merger", the combining should be accomplished without hiccup, and service delivery should be seamless. The partnering should capture all the benefits of rationalization and of the systems and process integration and consolidation, while retaining the loyalty and effectiveness of the employees of both institutions. The functions and systems should meld together and an entirely new culture should form – adopting the best characteristics of both.

Communication

Be candid, open and use good face-to-face communication. It also helps to establish rapport and pave the ground for new ideas when people admit the shortcomings in their previous methods and approaches. A key ingredient of the merger is that it must have a rational basis that is easy to explain and whose logic is powerful, succinct and irrefutable. It is absolutely critical when it comes to getting personnel to support, endorse and carry through the transaction at all levels, despite the turmoil and possible glitches it may create in their careers.

Process - Speed of Decision Making and Integration

The press report on IBM and PwC merger stated that the integration communication would be completed in two months flat! Large organizations completing such a mammoth job is commendable considering the fact that this has to be addressed at multi-location and multiple business groups. Slowness creates uncertainty and uncertainty, especially in a stressful environment of integrating a merger can be corrosive and eroding. Uncertainty also breeds conflicts. You will be better off making decisions quickly and later reversing mistakes, rather than letting decisions drag on too long (Dauphinais).

Handling People at Outplacement

Mergers create stress, discomfort, disruption and anxiety. This emotional atmosphere will get a great deal worse if the unemployed are not treated with fairness and compassion and if their abilities are not given the proper respect. One should go the extra mile to be responsive to the emotional needs of those who stayed on: first, by making sure that the logic of the transaction was perceived deep down and second, through communication programmes designed around employee preferences.

PROGNOSIS

Globally, there is a lull, as companies seem to have lost their appetite for buying out other companies. And the story is pretty much the same in India. Is it because of perceived mismatch and resultant problems between partners or an offshoot of general economic recession or due to depressed economic activity, most likely on account of fallout of 11 September 2001? Based on the data from Dealogic, KPMG Corporate Finance reports, the significant sectors for cross border merger activity in India in the first half of 2002 include automobiles, petroleum and gas, financial services, software / telecom and pharmaceuticals. Considering the hardships faced by many software companies, there is scope for more mergers for the sake of acquisition – clients and talents.

Mckinsey article on "Why Mergers Fail?" has advocated, "...Companies first look after their existing customers and revenue, retain their revenue generating talent and tailor the integration to balance their revenue and cost initiatives".

Merger Proficiency Model

Prophecy is that merged companies need the right people; we need them with set of competencies matching their organizational drivers, potential problems faced (Refer: Table 1) and whether the organization has resorted to mergers and acquisitions for tactical reasons or strategic and tactical reasons or for establishing a culture of continuous renewal and progress. We require different type of a leaders for managing these different merger objectives. Hence, need to develop a Merger Proficiency Model. A broad indication could be like Performance Competencies (for achieving the business imperatives of success in primary business objective – manufacturing, software or product development and financial performance), Relationship Competencies (for customer and employees satisfaction and retention), Managerial Competencies (for building effectiveness and quality processes within; developing knowledge diffusion, learning and people growth; building credibility inside and outside the organization) and Leadership competencies (for achieving business growth through deep investment in Research and Development, looking beyond today and initiating efforts that would impact every facet of human life; and institutionalizing practises within the organization) that would build a culture of continuous renewal and progress.

Bibliography

Business World, India, "Short of Breath", 29 July 2002, p 12 – 13

Curtis Bill, Hefley E William and Miller Sally., *People Capability Maturity Model (PCMM), Version 2*, SEI, Carnegie Mellon University, USA.

Dauphinais G William and Price Colin, *Straight From The CEO*, Price Waterhouse Coopers, USA, 1999.

Feros J.N., Lewis.A.F: *Mergers Are People*, Commerce Clearing House, Australia, 1979.

Geus Arie de, *The Living Company*, HBS, USA, 1997

Jones Robert and Oliver Marriott, *Anatomy of a Merger: A History of G.E.C., A.E.I and English Electric*, Cape, London, 1970

Kaipa, Prasad, "DNA Mapping Approach to M & A Scenarios", SelfCorp, Inc, USA, 2001 (White paper)

Premji Azim, "The New Economic Drivers", on constant change, Economic Times, 4th July 2002.

Pfeiffer Eckhard, "Future Tilt – How and Why Companies Need a Culture of Continuous Renewal?" a chapter in the book "Straight from the CEO", edited by Dauphinais G William and Price Colin, PWC, USA, 1999, Pg: 141 – 147.

Tichy Noel M and Sherman, Stratford, Control Your Destiny or Someone Else Will, Harper Business, New York, 1994.

The McKinsey Quarterlies at www.mckinseyquarterly.com

Water Shipley, "The Art of the Inclusive Merger", a chapter in the book "Straight from the CEO", edited by Dauphinais G William and Price Colin, PWC, USA, 1999, Pg: 207 - 212

Table 1 Merger Snapshot on Objectives, Drivers, Problems and Proposal

	Short-Term	Medium-Term	Long-Term
Scenario	Immediate and core	Beyond today & business operations	Impacts every facet of human life
Strategic Objectives	Post merger growth	Technological possibilities	Quality products and lowest cost using state of the art technology
	Global company requires presence in emerging market		
Drivers	Arbitrage opportunities	Geo-Political and WTC	To achieve industry lowest cost
		Acquire technology or domain or service expertise	Increase / lead customer service
			Leadership in product quality
E.g.:	Indian Software Industry	Godrej – GE in India	GE in USA
Problems	People wear their masks	Limited success in service	Cultural shift
	Cost synergy vs. revenue momentum	Not much on product ideas	Integration issues
Customer Front	Serving today's customer	Serving today's customers while developing tomorrows' customers	Identify products and services required for tomorrow
Knowledge Sharing	Activities copies without soul or spirit	Knowledge sharing at surface level and not at tacit level	Integrated team work to find solution to future economy and business
Proposal	Tactical – strengthen and grow core business	Strategic and tactical	Culture of continuous renewal & progress

CHAPTER

8

rethinking rewards for business excellence

C PREM KUMAR*

* C Prem Kumar, is Manager HR with Titan Industries Ltd., Bangalore.

Employee rewards and recognition are the critical areas of concern for increasing employee commitment. Study on various rewards / recognition mechanisms which will increase the employee commitment was conducted among the line managers with great emphasis on performance enhancement behaviour .Outcome of the survey is presented in this paper. Various recommendations were also listed out. Emphasis is on a simple but sincere recognition system as a potent tool for achieving **business excellence thorough employee commitment.**

Employee rewards is about how people are rewarded in accordance with their value to an organization. It is concerned with both financial and non-financial rewards and embraces the philosophies, strategies, policies , plans, processes used by organization to develop and maintain rewards system. (Figure 1)

In a recent survey of 378 companies summarized in HR focus (September 1998) noted that turnover rates continue to hold around 15 %. More alarmingly, the data indicated that the individuals most likely to leave an organization were from critical areas such as Information Technology, Sales, Marketing, and Customer Service.

Although these figures seem daunting, reducing costly turnover and driving up employee commitment and loyalty may not be as expensive and difficult as it would appear. Data from a recently released study from the Hay group indicates that factors such as recognitions for a job well done, respectful treatment and coaching and feedback were considered more important than pay in terms of employee commitment. Survey findings such as these have strong implication for effective leadership and management of people in today's business excellence scenario.

There are two basic types of rewards that leaders can utilize to positively reinforce performance enhancing behaviours. The first is money, certainly pay plays an integral positive behaviour, however often overlooked is the importance of providing employees with non financial rewards such as recognition and attention. This second type of rewards can be very effective and efficient because it does not cost much. It is available for every one to use and no one gets too much of it.

An informal survey was conducted for this article examining the importance of employee recognition in manufacturing organizations. Survey findings further provide support for the importance of recognition in manufacturing organization. It also indicates the importance of recognizing individuals for their work contribution. Outcome of the survey revealed strong support for the increased need for recognition throughout the organization.

First question asked was, if there was an increased need to be recognized for their work contribution .96 % of the respondents overwhelmingly supported this idea which indicated an increased need for recognition was necessary.

Recommendations One: For more effective leadership, in this organization and others there would be a need to increase the use of non-financial rewards by using creative techniques of recognize employees for outstanding contribution as, often as possible.

Next question required the respondents to judge the criteria for which someone should be recognized .Respondents rated Quality (81%) Performance (72%), Work contribution (66%), Service/Seniority (65%) & Others (13%). A sampling of the written comments falling in the "other" category included being recognized for attendance, outstanding work, timely response and resolution of problems, customers' service, adding value, exemplary demonstration of work ethic and willing to be cross –trained with other departments.

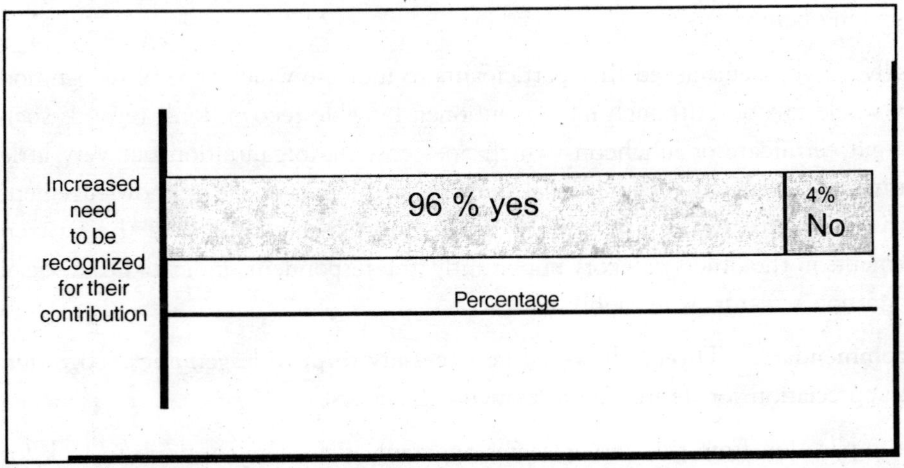

Figure 1 Survey Results

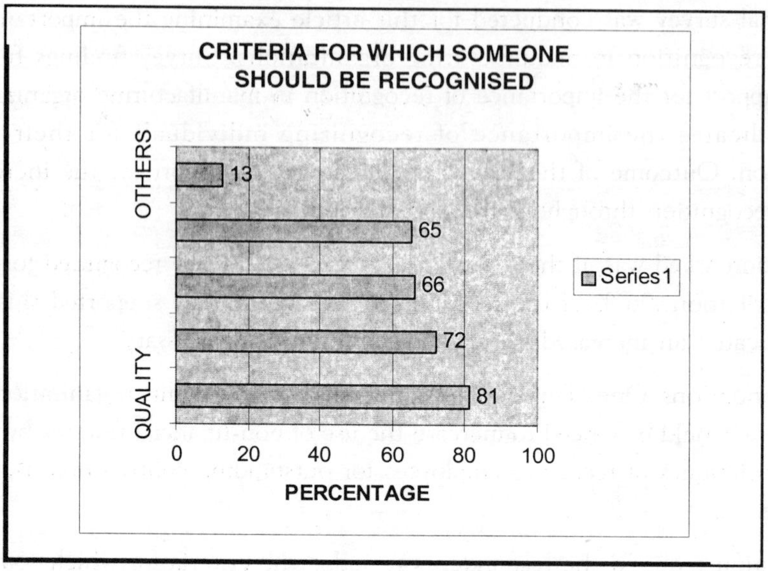

Figure 2

Interestingly, in this unionized environment, length of work service was not ranked as high as other performance based criteria.

Recommendation Two: Leader should base recognition /rewards not on mundane length of service or subjective factors, but more on objective, performance – enhancing behaviours.

Finally, survey items asked the participants to indicate which type of recognition they would favour .Although most mentioned tangible recognitions, rewards such as a gift certificate or luncheon which does cost the organization but very little relative to pay incentives and equal number mentioned public acknowledgement in the newsletter was sufficient. However, most interesting were the written comments in the others category importantly ,the respondents indicated that social recognition rewards were highly valued.

Recommendation Three: It would be necessary to provide genuine recognition and appreciation for desired performance behaviours.

The implication from this survey seems apparent, as leaders continue to look for ways to meet productivity, motivation and retention challenges of today for business excellence. The increased recognition of their human resources must be on primary importance. The message here is not to diminish or detract from the importance of other types of rewards such as monetary incentives. Further, the research and the supporting survey results, point out that important, but often overlooked. Simple but sincere recognitions / rewards work as a potent tool for business excellence in today's context.

Table 1 Examples of Non –Monetary Recognitions

CERTIFICATE OF RECOGNITIONS
GIFT CERTIFICATES NOT EXCHANGEABLE FOR CASH
LUNCH / DINNER
FLOWER BASKET
TICKETS TO VARIOUS EVENTS
FUNNY T -SHIRTS
HUMOROUS ITEMS (COFFEE MUGS, PEN STAND)
CD's
LIBRARY MEMBERSHIPS

References:

Alderfer.C. (1972) Existence, Relatedness Growth, New York, Free Press

MCGRECOG D. (1960) The Human Side of Enterprise, New York,

McGraw -Hill

MacMillian K (1988) Perks in Perspective, Henky Management College, Henky.

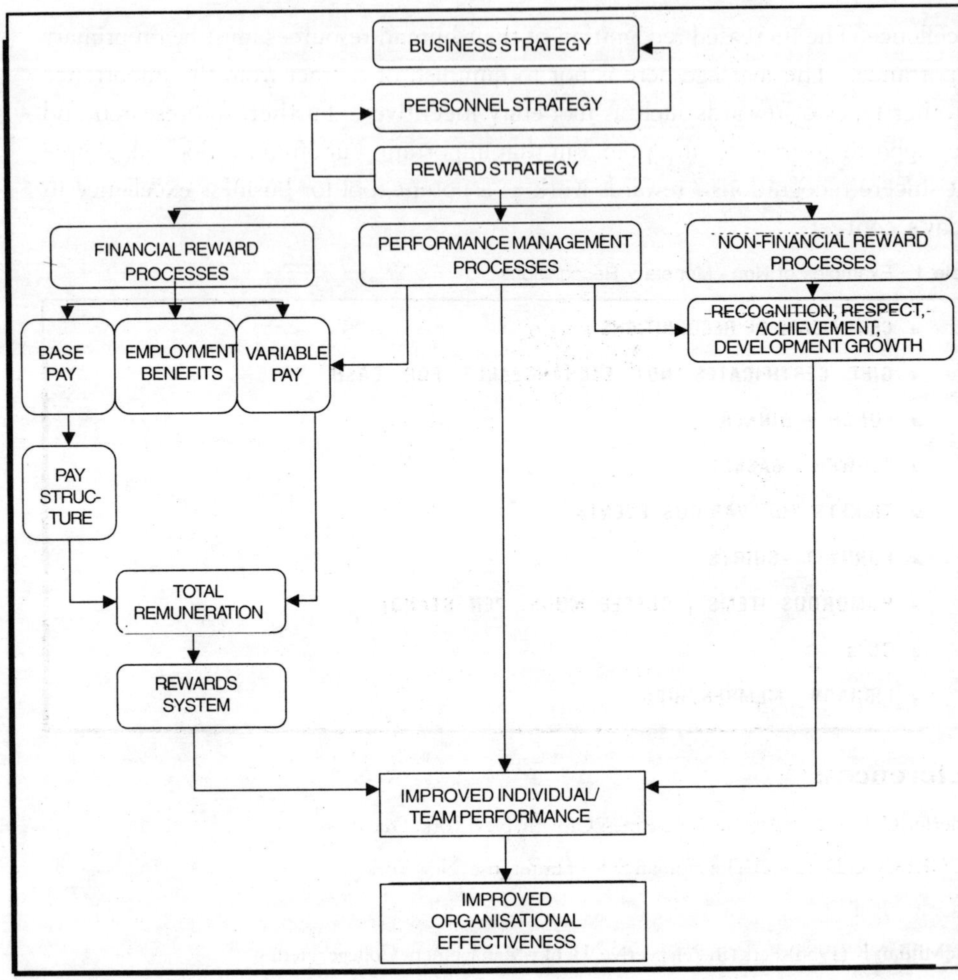

Figure 3 The Reward System

►HR Processes for Value Addition◄

CHAPTER 9

creating value through competency mapping and assessment

J JACOB AND ROOPASHREE SHANKAR*

* J Jacob and Roopashree Shankar are consultants with Feedback Reach Consultancy, an HR consulting firm.

INTRODUCTION

The current organizational environment is changing as companies increasingly focus on human capital as a competitive advantage. To achieve business success, companies are expecting their employees to perform at higher levels, to be more customer-responsive, more process-oriented, more involved in shared leadership and more responsible for creating the knowledge that adds value to an organization's distinguishing capabilities. Organizations, meanwhile, are becoming leaner as they align themselves with other companies to achieve their business strategy and maintain core values.

In order to accomplish any of these objectives, HR professionals must be able to help their organizations identify and grow required employee competencies. It is now a leading organizational strategy to apply competencies in all major HR areas, including recruitment, selection, assessment, development, appraisal, and rewards.

In a demanding and changing work environment, the merits of a competency-based HRM system becomes even more valuable. Tasks and jobs are becoming less useful methods of describing the work of individuals and organizations. People and competencies are proving to be a more appropriate unit of analysis. They are also a more valuable method for describing work and the strengths and the weaknesses of individuals and organizations. In the future, organizations will be built around this form of analysis.

Competencies are generally defined as groupings of behaviours that encompass the knowledge, skills, attitudes, motives, and temperaments that distinguish excellent performers. A competency focuses on how an employee creates value and what is actually accomplished. In other words, competencies answer the question – "What does an excellent performer look like in a particular work setting?"

COMPETENCIES FOR COMPETITIVE ADVANTAGE

Human capital is the ultimate weapon for achieving competitive advantage. Nowhere is it more powerfully illustrated than in the saga of highly successful organizations worldwide who have achieved market leadership by systematically identifying, developing, rewarding and aligning people competencies with their unique differentiating organizational capabilities.

The need to link the intellectual capital of the firm to the strategic objectives is the order of the day. Firms have realized that unless they align themselves accordingly they will not be able to gain a competitive advantage. Thus, a competency-based approach is today being used by a lot many organizations in achieving their strategic objectives.

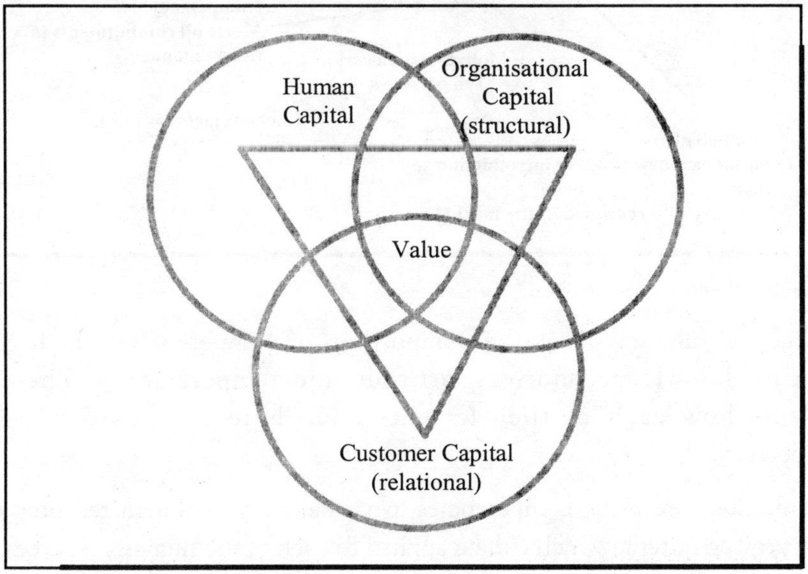

Figure 1

The diagram above explains the relationship between human capital (competencies), organizational capital and customer capital, all of which are needed in the creation of value.

Thus, a competency model is a set of success factors, often called competencies that include key behaviours required for excellent performance in a particular role. These behaviours are demonstrated by superior performers on the job.

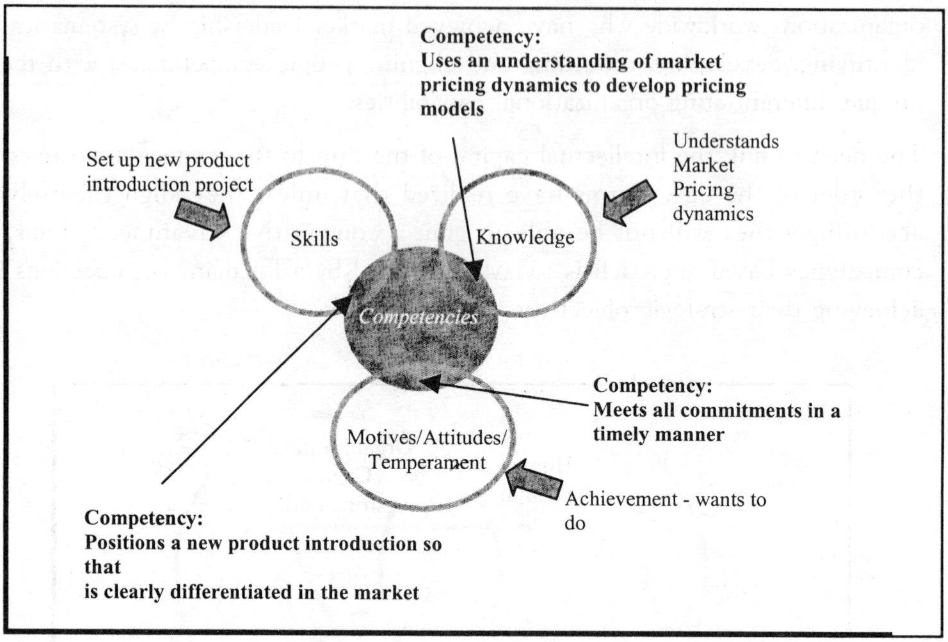

Figure 2

The above diagram shows the composition of competencies which comprise of skills, knowledge, motives, attitude and temperament. The diagram explains how each of the elements contribute towards determining a competency.

Organizations are using competencies in virtually every human resource domain. They provide criteria, which can be applied to each of the human resource practises shown below:

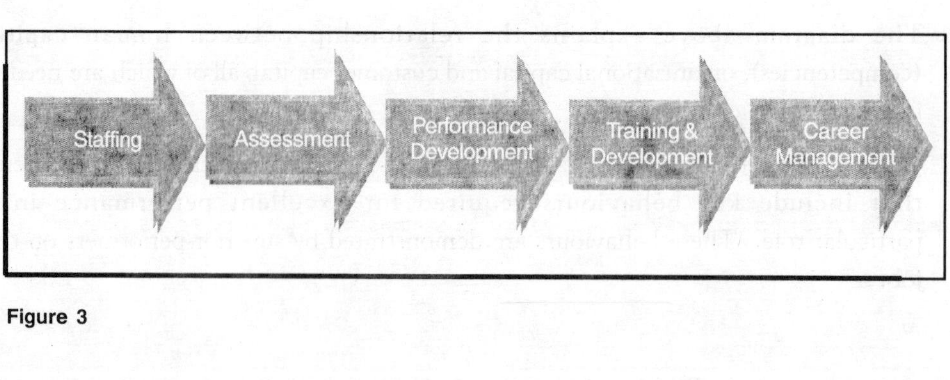

Figure 3

Case Study

Feedback reach was commissioned by a Fortune 500 organization to assist them in a competency mapping and assessment exercise. Feedback worked with the organization over a period of 4 months in the design and implementation of the system. The essence of the assignment was in ensuring that this initiative contributed to enhancing performance across the organization.

The assignment is unfolded as a case study in the following pages:

Competency Mapping and Assessment: A Case Study at a Fortune 500 Organization

Brief Background

The organization is into the manufacturing of crude and refined oil and has been in operation close to a century. In an era where rapid growth and its sustenance is the key to success, the organization as part of its planned initiatives was in the process of implementing a SAP programme which would integrate all functions, across the organization for improved efficiencies. The necessity of HR to be integrated across functions was imminent for the organization taking into account the size and growth of the organization.

The organization as part of its continuing efforts to achieve excellence in human development practises was embarking on a new initiative of implementing the HR module of SAP and documenting a profile catalogue for senior management positions through profiling of competencies for benchmark / key roles.

The broad objectives of the assignment were to :

(a) develop competency profiles for benchmark positions (Approx 40) at the senior management level and,

(b) define a set of behavioural indicators for the benchmark positions which would ultimately lead to superior performance .

The end purpose of the exercise was to put in place a system of identification and profiling of competencies for individual roles which would help in:

- Aligning people competencies with unique and differentiating organizational capabilities of the organization.

- Enable the organization to reinforce corporate strategy, culture and vision, establish expectations for performance excellence and provide common organization wide standards for career progression that enables employees to move within and across functional & divisional boundaries.
- Help the organization not only to identify knowledge / skill deficiencies in employees but also recognize their achievements, identify employees who are focused, energized and are superior performers.

FEEDBACK REACH'S APPROACH TO THE ASSIGNMENT

A comprehensive process for mapping competencies at the individual level was developed to reinforce organizational capabilities for superior performance. This unique process, called "Integrated Competency Approach for Superior Performance"

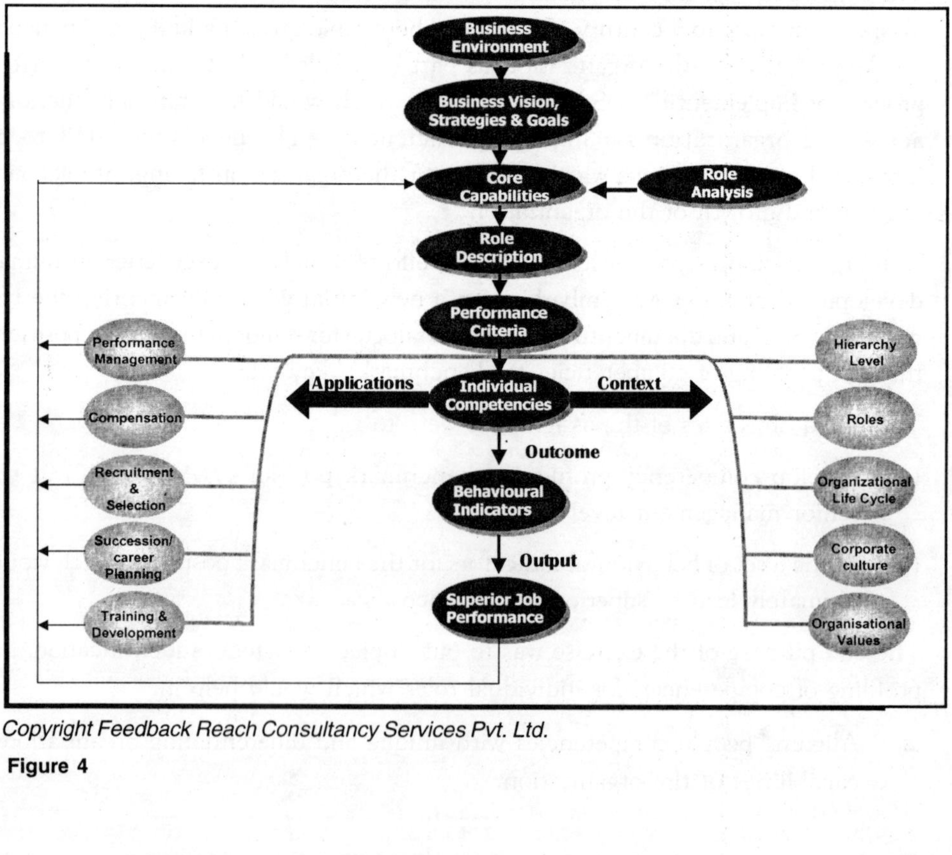

Copyright Feedback Reach Consultancy Services Pvt. Ltd.

Figure 4

provides a vertical link between people and business, and horizontal integration amongst key HR systems (such as compensation, performance management, selection, career and succession planning, etc.) to best leverage them in the creation of value.

Sequential Stages in the Model

The following four phases are involved in creating a competency profile:

1. **Selecting** the relevant competency categories and competency clusters and listing the relevant individual competencies.
2. **Determining** the relative importance of each competency listed, by weight or rank ordering.
3. **Identifying** specific effective and ineffective behavioural expressions of each competency listed - this is often referred to as creating behavioural indicators.
4. **Determining** the required or actual level of mastery of each competency listed.

The above four stages integrate people and their roles.

Methodology Adopted for the Assignment

The methodology, which was developed, has been illustrated in the following flow diagram.

The methodology involved extensive and in-depth interviews with the role holders (of benchmark positions) and large networks of their internal and external stakeholders. The strategic requirements of the organization were derived from its business goals and strategies and disaggregated into individual benchmark roles.

Following the above steps, a first cut of the competency profile was developed. This involved the selection of competency categories, competency clusters, and individual competencies for all the benchmark positions. The next step involved gathering additional supporting information. Based on this information, the profile was reviewed, tailored and finalized. At this time, the relative importance of each competency was established. Finally, the level of mastery was determined for each competency listed and associated behavioural expressions were created and refined.

Creating a Competency Profile

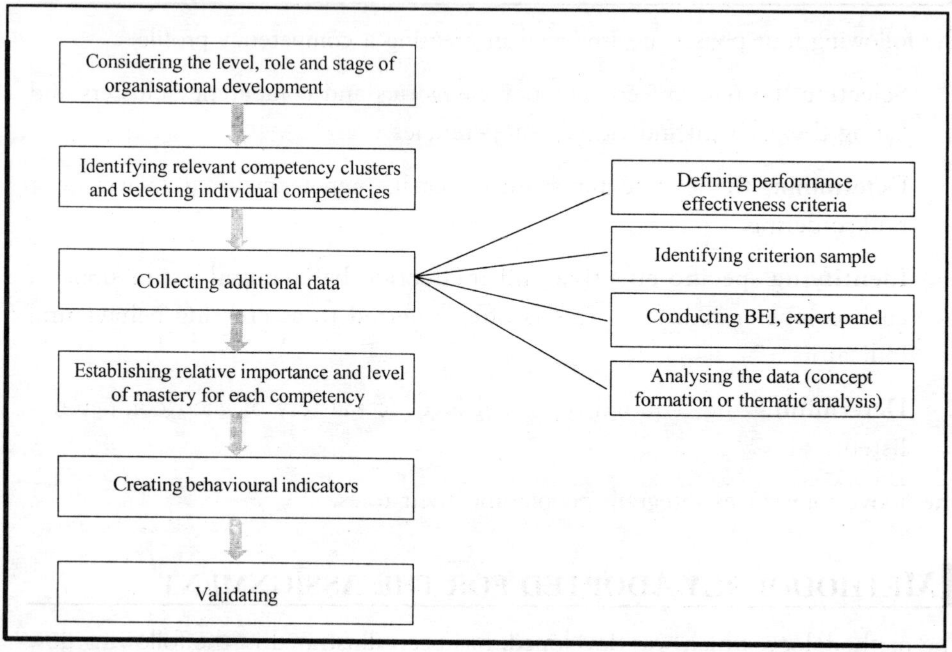

Source: Spencer & Spencer

Figure 5

How Did We Go About Doing the Assignment?

The organization had role descriptions for the benchmark positions, which needed to be updated. Our first step was to freeze the role description as the starting point to competency mapping. We used a process driven approach by identifying a network of stakeholders for each role holder and understanding their expectations from the role holder. Having taken into account the expectations of each stakeholder and the role holder offerings, the role was finalized through a role negotiation process. Each stakeholder had to also state the support to be provided to the role holder for the performance of the role. These were known as boundary conditions. The next step was to detail out the Measures of Performance (MOPs) or the "What of Performance' for each role in the organization. Performance of the individual was measured using the Balanced Scorecard Approach taking into account financial, customer driven, business processes, and learning & growth perspectives. Therefore, each individual's contribution was measured on these perspectives.

Having detailed out the "What of Performance", the next logical step was in determining the "How of Performance" - in essence, the competencies required to deliver the "What of Performance".

The organizational vision was analysed in depth to cull out organizational competencies required by all role holders in contributing towards achievement of the organizational vision. Detailed analysis of the hierarchy level of the role, the culture and values of the organization were looked at to assess organizational and specific level related competencies.

The main input towards the competency mapping exercise was the Behavioural Event Interview (BEI) technique, which is a tested method of identifying competencies. The purpose of the behavioural event interview is to get behind what people say they do, to find out what they really do. This is accomplished by asking people to describe how they actually behaved in specific incidents.

We conducted behavioural event interviews with each role holder to get very detailed behavioural descriptions of how the role holder goes about doing his / her work. We asked questions to role holders to enable them to narrate critical incident short stories.

The objective was to get the role holder to describe in detail at least three critical incidents detailing out what the situation was, who all were involved, what did the role holder feel at that point of time, what did the role holder think about others, and what was the outcome.

We conducted BEIs with other individuals who had earlier held the role holder's position. This process was undertaken in order to gauge the correlation between the BEIs. The other role holders were both average and superior performers.

Manuscripts were analysed in detail to arrive at competency clusters and differentiating behavioural indicators. Thus, the deliverables to the client were:

- Updation of "role descriptions" for benchmark roles. This involved revision of role descriptions already available with them.
- Defining a clear set of "measures of performance" for the above roles.
- "mapping competencies" of the benchmark. Roles that support and reinforce organizational capabilities, giving due consideration to organization structure and environment variables such as role, level and stage of organizational development.
- Defining a set of "behavioural indicators" for benchmark positions leading to a superior performance
- Determining the "relative importance" and required "level of mastery" for each of the competencies.

The entire process required classification of competencies into the relative categories and culling out behavioural indicators, which are observable and measurable.

ASSESSMENT OF COMPETENCIES

However, identifying the competencies that are essential for individuals in an organization to effectively carry out their roles is just the first step towards ensuring the organization's success. Equally important, is to measure the extent to which individuals within the organization possess the required competencies. One of the ways of doing this is to take the individuals, whose competencies need to be assessed, through a development/assessment centre. This is a very powerful process for assessing the abilities of participants against an agreed set of success criteria for a job or role. The origins of the assessment centre lie in the period before Second World War, when it was used for selection of British and German officers. The method began to get off the ground in the forties, primarily in United States, and by the late fifties was being further developed by the business community, in particular by the American Telephone & Telegraph Company (AT&T). Since 1970, the assessment centre method has grown into a force to be reckoned with in the United States and in Europe.

At the client organization, we decided to take the participants through a development centre rather than an assessment centre. Though both processes are designed to measure the abilities of the participants, the primary difference between the two is that development centres are used to identify the personal development and training needs of people either in their current role or for a future role, whereas assessment centres are used for selecting job applicants.

Some key characteristics of this process are as follows:

1. Observations in the centre are based on key dimensions or competencies that differentiate between successful and less successful performance.
2. Observations are arrived at by a skills analysis, which may include the following methods:
   a) Interviewing managers performing the job about how they structure their time and which activities are critical.
   b) Observations about people doing the job.
   c) Collecting a wide range of information by the use of an appropriately designed job analysis questionnaire.
3. Development centres measure the abilities of participants by simulating a job or role situation that requires them to demonstrate abilities in the relevant competencies.
4. Exercises are designed according to certain criteria:
   a) The ability of the exercise to bring out the required behaviour.
   b) The level of education, ability and experience of the participants.
   c) The relative importance of the different competencies based on the job content of the target job or role.
   d) The need to observe the participants in a variety of situations.
   e) The need to observe the demonstration of competencies in different exercises.
   f) The time and resources available for the centre.
5. Rating of participant performance is undertaken by trained assessors.

6. The process involves one-to-one feedback interviews with participants, during which the strengths & development areas that have been highlighted by performance on the centre are discussed. Data that have been collected by the trained assessors may also be pooled with those produced prior to the centre by peers, subordinates, and line managers, who have completed job performance questionnaires/ 360 degree feedback for the participant.

7. Assessor's assessments are collated and distilled into a written report before the one-to-one feedback interview. This, often involves a plenary discussion in which assessors who have assessed the same individual in different exercises discuss the overall performance of that individual by reviewing all of the evidence.

As the client organization, after identifying the competencies essential for success at the senior management level, we charted a process for assessing those competencies. The entire process is explained below.

The Process

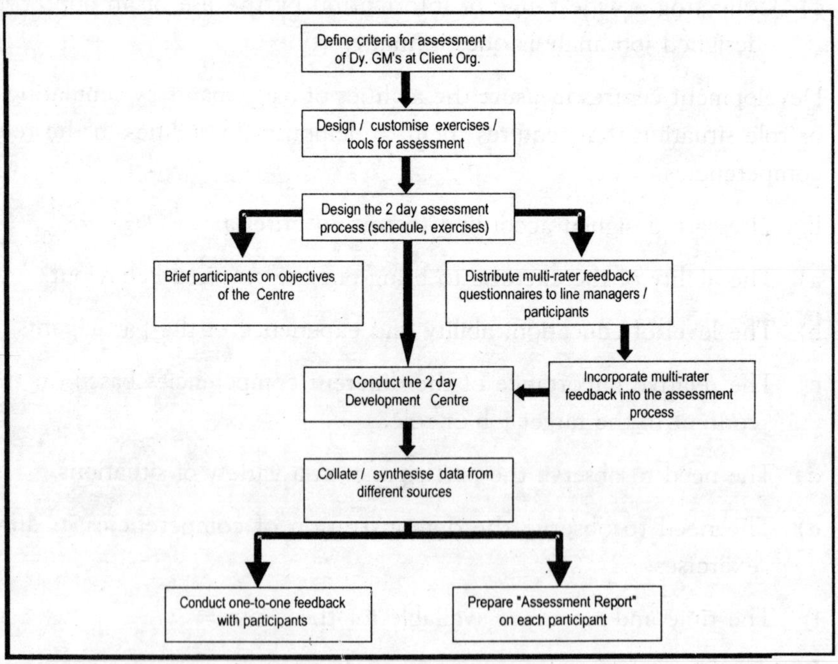

Figure 6

After completion of the first stage of the assignment, we had lists of competencies for the various levels of management in the organization. However, it was decided that first only the senior management (DGMs) would undergo the assessment process. In consultation with the client, it was decided that the purpose of the centre would be developmental in nature and the output would be used primarily for charting out development plans for the participants.

Around 45 DGMs were identified who would undergo this exercise. The relevant competencies were chosen on which the participants would be assessed. There were 10 competencies in all that were felt to be necessary for superior performance at the DGM level in the organization.

The subsequent step was to design exercises to measure these competencies. For this, it was essential to identify positive and negative behaviours corresponding to each competency. Based on the identified behaviours, exercises and tests were designed. While designing the exercises, we had to keep in mind that they should be able to bring out the behaviours relevant to different competencies to be measured, which could then be observed, recorded, and then analysed. For each of the exercises, observer sheets were also prepared. The observer sheet had a description of the competencies that were to be measured through the exercise, a list of positive and negative behaviours associated with the competencies, and space for assessors to write their comments. The added advantage of the observer sheet was that frequencies could also be recorded i.e. every time a participant exhibited a particular behaviour, whether positive or negative, related with the competencies to be measured, it would be recorded by the assessors. Thus, at the end of the exercise, we would have data on not only behaviours (related to different competencies) that were exhibited by the different participants but also how often those behaviours were exhibited.

Another important step was to train the assessors and brief them on the exercises and what they were expected to observe and record. As there were six assessors in all, it was imperative that they all have similar understanding of the process, competencies, exercises, and how and what to observe, record, and evaluate. This was the only way that we could guarantee consistency in the approach and evaluation by different assessors.

A 360 degree feedback questionnaire was prepared and mailed to all the participants and their peers, subordinates, and superiors. The questionnaire consisted of various items related to the competencies to be measured. The objective of this questionnaire was to gauge the performance of the participants on various dimensions from their key stakeholder's perspectives within the organization, understand the gaps, if any, that exist between the individual's self perception and those of others, as well as list the strengths and areas of improvement of each individual. The completed questionnaires were received well before the start of the development centre. They were analysed and a brief report was prepared on each participant based on the ratings that they received on the various dimensions.

After all the exercises and tests were ready, we designed a two day development centre. The template is provided in the annexure. Since there were around 45 DGM's to be assessed, five separate centres were held and each had approximately 9 participants.

Each centre was inaugurated by the Executive Director of the organization. The intention was to convey the seriousness of the organization towards this intervention as well as allay the fears and doubts that the participants might have since this exercise was being carried out for the very first time in the history of the organization. At the start of each centre, a half an hour introductory session was held to explain the purpose of the development centre to the participants, brief them about the schedule for two days and what they are expected to do, and also share with them how the results from the development centre would be used by the organization. The participants were then taken through a series of exercises that consisted of role plays, in-basket, case studies, personality assessment tools etc. Each exercise was designed in such a way that:

a) each competency was tested from atleast two different exercises. This was important for enhancing the quality and accuracy of the evidence. And,

b) assessors were not overloaded by asking them to obtain evidence against too many competencies during an exercise.

Since the objective of the centre was developmental in nature, the assessors provided feedback to the participants during the course of the centre also. Towards the end of the session, a one-to-one feedback session was arranged between the participants and the assessors. During this session, results from the 360 degree feedback was shared with the participants which helped them gain a better insight into how their performance is perceived by others on various dimensions, what their inherent strengths are, and which are the areas that need further development.

Based on the assessment data flowing from different exercises, reports were prepared on every participant highlighting their strengths and areas of improvement, and how they performed vis-à-vis the different competencies. The participants were also rated on a 10 point scale on each of the competencies. Thus, it became possible to compare the performance of the participants on different competencies.

The final report on the participants was sent across to the HR department to enable them to plan developmental interventions for the DGMs.

LIMITATIONS OF THE PROCESS

Our effort was to make the entire process as objective as possible. However, it is quite possible that a certain degree of subjectivity can creep in. This can especially happen during the observation and recording of behaviour by the assessors. To eliminate this, the assessors should not try and interpret data but restrict themselves to only recording what they observe.

We also noticed that during the feedback process some participants go on the defensive if their 360 degree feedback had not been positive, or if they had not performed well in some of the exercises. In such a situation, it is important for the assessors to handle the participants skillfully and ensure that the participants remain receptive and open to suggestions and feedback. The purpose of the centre would be defeated if the participants are unable to realize their shortcomings and understand where they need to improve.

Ideally, a development centre should be held for three to four days. Sufficient amount of time needs to be devoted for providing in depth feedback to the participants after each exercise. However, we were operating under a time crunch and had to restrict the duration of the centre to just two days. Because of the time constraint, we feel that the participants were not able to reap the full benefits of the process.

EPILOGUE

Inspite of certain shortcomings, the entire intervention was viewed as a positive step taken by the organization towards achieving its goals and proved to be beneficial for the participants also. The process was a learning experience for us too. We realized that we should have invested more time in giving one-to-one feedback to the participants on their performance in the different exercises, and how they could improve their performance on certain dimensions.

There are also valuable learnings for organizations who are interested in carrying out this process, and for participants who would like to attend such a centre.

For Organizations

It is very important for an organization to be clear about the objectives of undertaking such an intervention. If the objective is the development of their employees then they should be willing to invest necessary time and resources in the process. Secondly, there has to be transparency in the process. Ideally, the final report should be shared with the participants and their line managers to enable them to chart out development plans. However, this was not done in this case as the client was not comfortable in sharing the data. Also, the purpose of holding the centre needs to be communicated clearly to the participants and their line managers. In this particular case, many participants came to the centre with a lot of anxiety. They were not clear about the purpose of attending the centre and how the outcome would affect decisions regarding their promotions, job rotations, transfers etc. Though in the introductory session an attempt was made to lessen their anxiety, all their queries could not be addressed because of various constraints and this could have adversely affected their performance.

For Participants

If the participants wish to perform well then they have to be receptive and attend the centre with an open mind. A defensive attitude is a huge barrier in the development process. They need to understand that this process is not aimed at finding out who is a good or bad performer but at bringing out each individual's inherent strengths and weaknesses. Once they are aware of their weaknesses they can chart out a development plan in consultation with their superiors to enhance their performance.

This process is an effective tool in the hands of organizations who are serious about enhancing performance provided it is carried out properly. The true success of this intervention would depend on how well the organization can utilize the results obtained and enhance the performance of the participants on the job, thereby enhancing organizational performance.

ANNEXURE

DEVELOPMENT CENTRE PROGRAMME
XYZ LIMITED
19th DECEMBER, 2001
Programme Schedule

TIME		SESSION
DAY - 1 (19-12-2001)		
0930 - 0950	• Welcome GM (HR)	
	• Inauguration ED (HR)	
	• Objectives Feedback Reach -	
0950 - 1030	Icebreaker - (Open Space)	
1030 - 1050	Reflection & Processing - (Open Space)	
1050 - 1135	Case - (Individual work)	Group Exercise (Simultaneous Individual Work)
	(Participants 1,2,3,4,5)	(Participants 6,7,8,9,10)
1135 - 1205	Presentation & Discussion	Reflection & Processing
	(1,2) (3,4) (5,6)	
1205 - 1220	Tea Break	
1220 - 1305	Group Exercise (Simultaneous Individual Work)	Case - (Individual work)
	(Participants 1,2,3,4,5)	(Participants 6,7,8,9,10)
1305 - 1330	Reflection & Processing	Presentation & Discussion (6,7) (8,9) (10)
1330 - 1415	Lunch Break	
1415 - 1525	Role Play (Participants 1,2,3,4,5)	Role Play (Participants 6,7,8,9,10)
1525 - 1625	Outdoor Exercise followed by reflection and processing	
1625 - 1640	Tea Break	
1640 - 1740	In-Basket (Individual work)	
1740 - 1800	In Basket - Discussions & Learning	

DEVELOPMENT CENTRE PROGRAMME
XYZ LIMITED
20th DECEMBER, 2001
Programme Schedule

TIME	SESSION			
DAY - 2 (20-12-2001)				
0930 - 1000	Reflection & Learning			
1000 - 1130	Personality Assessment Tool (Processing & Learning)			
1130 - 1145	Tea Break			
1145 - 1325	Negotiation Exercise (Individual work followed by Group work and Inter-group Negotiations)			
	Group - 1 (1,2,3,4,5)			
	Group - 2 (6,7,8,9,10)			
1325 - 1410	Lunch Break			
1410 - 1455	Individual Feedback	Psychometric Test	BEI	Small Group Exercise
	(Participants 1,2,3)	(Participants 4,5,6)	(Participants 7,8,)	(Participants 9,10)
1455 - 1540	Individual Feedback	Psychometric Test	BEI	Small Group Exercise
	(Participants 4,5,6)	(Participants 1,2,3)	(Participants 9,10)	(Participants 7,8)
1540 - 1555	Tea Break			
1555 - 1640	Individual Feedback	Psychometric Test	BEI	Small Group Exercise
	(Participants 7,8)	(Participants 9,10)	(Participants 1,2,3)	(Participants 4,5,6)
1640 - 1725	Individual Feedback	Psychometric Test	BEI	Small Group Exercise
	(Participants 9,10)	(Participants 7,8)	(Participants 4,5,6)	(Participants 1,2,3)
1725 - 1755	Individual Learning & Action Plan			
1755 - 1800	Closure			

CHAPTER

10

reinventing the organizational DNA

a new enquiry into 'the process' of development needs analysis

ARJUN SHEKHAR, MEENAL GUPTA AND SWEETY CHOPRA*

* Arjun Shekhar (Director), Meenal Gupta (Performance Support Partner) and Sweety Chopra (Performance Support Partner) from Vyaktitva, a Delhi based performance support - consulting firm that works towards performance enhancement of organizations.

What Kind of Wealth Grows When You Use it and Withers Away Under Lock and Key?

Knowledge or learning. As learning theorist David Kolb[1] has said, learning should result in a change in behaviour. Without walking it, the talk remains in the realm of the virtual. To make learning real you have to use it. Almost every time we conduct a first training program, this expectation comes out loud and clear from the participants, "Will we really use it back at our workplace?"

Take the case of Sumit, a junior manager in an automobile manufacturing major. He is attending his third Management Development Program (MDP). Sumit really wants to grow and impact the business in a big way; but his cynicism of training programmes as a tool for learning is apparent. He feels that the immediate reaction to these programmes is usually enthusiastic and sometimes there is a lot of learning also but when it comes to walking the talk on the shopfloor.... there is hardly any change in behaviour. Sumit and his co-participants are not being unjustly critical because most training has yet to prove its effectiveness on the shopfloor. But it would be unfair to the training fraternity to dismiss their efforts completely, for there is a value even in that initial enthusiasm. In fact, Donald Kirkpatrick's model[2] looks at effectiveness at different levels:

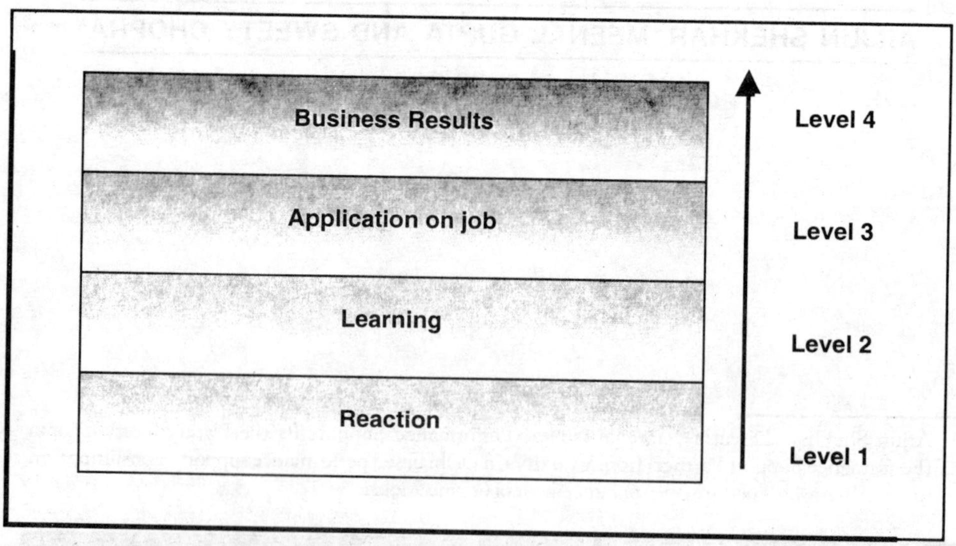

Figure 1 Kirkpatrick's Model of Evaluation of Training Effectiveness

- ***Reaction***: This first level of evaluation measures the participants' immediate satisfaction level with the programme content, materials, instructors, facilities, methodologies etc., typically captured on the training feedback form.

- ***Learning:*** The second level measures the extent to which the participants have absorbed the principles, facts, techniques and skills covered in the programme, typically evaluated using pre and post tests.

- ***Application on job:*** This third level is concerned with measuring how well the participants are able to apply the skills learned in the programme to their jobs, usually measured through peer and supervisor feedback and achievement of action plans made during the programme.

- ***Business results:*** The fourth level of evaluation involves monitoring quantifiable business results such as cost savings, work output changes, quality changes etc.

Jack J Phillips has added a **fifth level** to Kirkpatrick's Model; the ***ROI or the Return on Investment level*** [3], which compares the monetary benefits of the programme with its costs. The ratio of the programme's costs to its benefits (expressed as a percentage) is the return on investment of the programme.

Figure 2

Wonder what level of evaluation are they referring to!!!

On a more serious note, organizations worldover evaluate their training programme at different levels depending on the maturity level that the training function in these organizations has attained. Our research indicates that organizations like Dell Computer Corporation, Nortel, Bell Atlantic evaluate most of their training at the 4th Level viz. what are the business results from training programme [4]. Some have used Jack Phillips methodology to evaluate training at the 5th level. Dell Computer Corporation, for instance implemented a five-step ROI measurement process for their Sales Negotiation Training Program in 1997 and found that the ROI for a period of 3 months was 523.25%. The total net profit to the company was $763,297. Control and training groups were tested on specific business metrics both before and after the training programme and an overall improvement of 17.63% was calculated for the training group.

However most of the Indian companies have not reached that level of maturity yet. In a survey conducted by us, we found that most companies take formal post training feedback; while some conduct pre and post tests. The data thus collected is used for Level 1 and Level 2 evaluation of training programme. Few companies are able to evaluate Level 3 results through 360-degree feedback forms and shop floor project assignments. Only a handful of the companies we surveyed are in the process of designing a system for evaluating the quantitative business results from training.

Of course, all the companies surveyed talked of the need to do Level 4 evaluation of training. With so much media hype over the last decade, the buzzword of the new millennium has been *Integrating HR to Business*. Therefore, the need for evaluation of training and showing business results from training are the top management's demands that HR managers of professionally run companies dream to fulfill.

But we find even the handful of companies actually trying to achieve this dream wake up halfway in their efforts to find that although they have been making good progress on the ladder of training evaluation, the ladder itself is placed on the wrong wall. You can evaluate the benefits to individuals from a training programme on the shop floor and find major improvements but still the business results may not be forthcoming. Our contention is that almost always the blame can be laid on their design than their evaluation processes. We need to step back from the ladder to look at the very first step of Instruction Design viz. which wall to climb or what are the desired outcomes for a business from a training intervention. This, we believe, constitutes the DNA of a learning organization. Only an accurate Development Needs Analysis can transform training intervention outcomes to become aligned to business. Without unfolding the real DNA, the intervention will always be akin to firing from a shotgun - a spray of contents hoping that something will hit business targets.

Our intensive work in designing and implementing learning initiatives for different sectors of the Indian Industry led us to think that the answer for Indian organizations lies in *reinventing the Development Needs Analysis process rather than concentrating on evaluation of the results from training.* To reconfirm our hunch, we took a fresh look at the commonly followed process of Instruction Design.

THE INSTRUCTION DESIGN PROCESS REDEFINED

The commonly applied Instruction Design process follows the well-known ADDIE cycle:

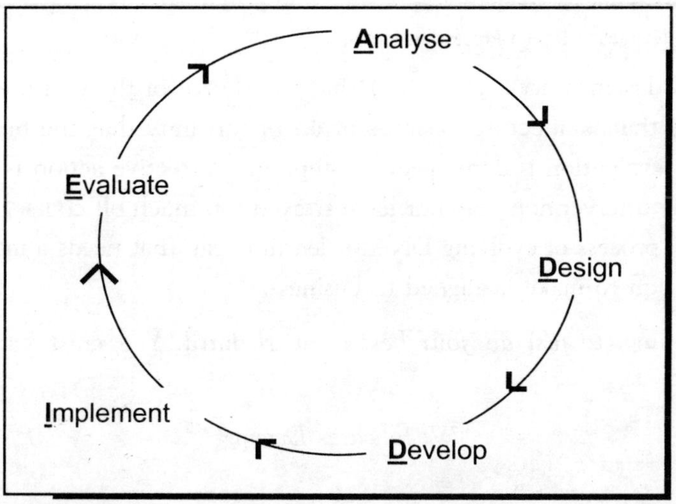

Figure 3 The ADDIE Model

In the above process, evaluation is done at the last stage like the traditional quality inspection conducted after the product has been made (in this case, even delivered).

Taking a leaf from the latest Quality Assurance Models, let us consider what if evaluation was to be done at each step of the Instruction Design process. Modified, the Instruction Design process would look something like this:

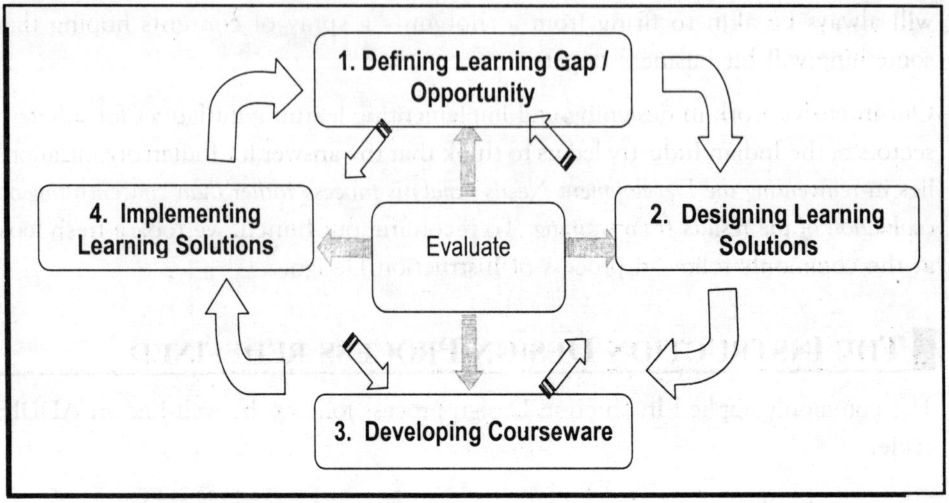

Figure 4 The Instruction Design Process Redefined

This revised design process ensures a) that the source of the entire exercise is a learning gap that is affecting business or an opportunity that the business must seize and b) evaluation is done at every step; any corrective action is taken early on, when the intervention may not have strayed too much off course. We believe that it is the process of evolving DNA or learning gap that needs a major enquiry and reinvention to make it aligned to business.

It is not enough to just do your best or work hard. You must know what to work on.

W. Edwards Deming

HOW DEVELOPMENT NEEDS ARE IDENTIFIED PRESENTLY

To understand the current practise of DNA, we surveyed companies from different business sectors like financial services, automobile manufacturers, FMCGs, call centres, insurance etc. across Delhi and Bangalore. We found that broadly, companies use the following process to arrive at their training calendars:

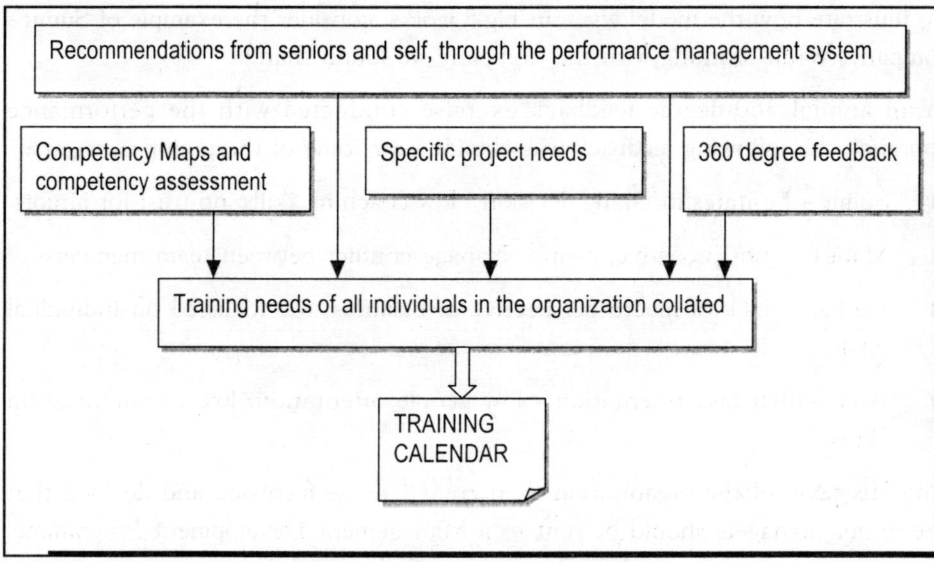

Figure 5 Present Training Need Identification Process

More specifically, the survey findings showed the following distribution of bases for identifying training needs:

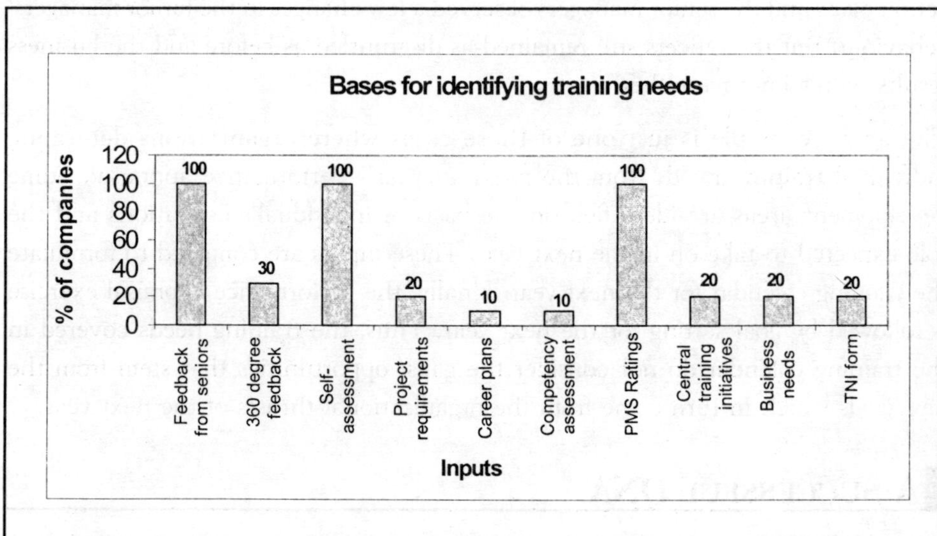

Figure 6 Present bases for identifying training needs

To illustrate how the model given in Fig.5 works, consider the example of Sumit's company. While working with this company we found that:

In an annual 360-degree feedback exercise conducted with the performance appraisal, the following feedback was obtained for some of the junior managers:

- Sumit – hesitates in taking decisions, low coaching skills, no trust for juniors.
- Manish – not proactive, cannot manage conflict between team members.
- Pankaj - lack of macro perspective of business, too focussed on individual goals.
- Amit –high task orientation - low people orientation, low communication skills.

The HR team of the organization then compiled the feedback and decided that the junior managers should be sent to a Management Development Programme. The programme, thus conducted, was very well received. Most managers were glad to get out of the factories for some time and get exposed to what they teach in business schools. At the end of the programme action plans were formulated. After a month of the first programme, a follow up was done to check the progress on the action plans and the senior managers observed a few changes in the junior managers' behaviour. But the officers still remained as disgruntled as before and the business results didn't improve either.

The above example is just one of those cases where organizations determine individual training needs from the previous year's performance appraisal. Some development areas are identified on the basis of individual's aspirations and the role expected to take on in the next year. These inputs are compiled to formulate the training calendar for the next year. Finally, the performance appraisal exercise is followed by goal setting for the next year. Thus, the training needs covered in the training calendar do not consider the gaps/ opportunities that stem from the new goals which in turn come from the organizational thrusts of the next year.

A SUCCESSFUL DNA

Now, consider the example of an international back office transaction processing company that was facing the problem of high attrition rate of process associates in a particular business unit. We were told that the attrition rates had risen by 8% in a period of 11 months. The senior management in the organization arrived at the following possible reasons from a root cause analysis:

- Insufficient job challenge
- Lack of feedback from the managers
- Desire for higher studies
- Dissatisfactory compensation structure
- Low managerial skills of the supervisors
- Lack of job enrichment opportunities
- Absence of career plans for the process associates

On being presented with the problem, we began with a voice of customer analysis where we met the senior team, the process associates and the HR team in order to understand their view of the problem. The feedback was then supplemented with the shop floor context. From these two inputs, we realized that the company offered excellent work environment, good remuneration and other motivational rewards, but the supervisors were not able to meet the individual growth expectations of the process associates. The learning gap thus isolated was "The inability of managers to take ownership of the aspirations of their team members". We, then designed a programme for enabling better management of team aspirations by the middle rung leaders, specifically customized to bringing down attrition. The objectives of the programme were:

- Identify improvement areas in own skills of :
  - rapport building for understanding team aspirations.
  - building agreement on possible career plans for team members.
- Apply potential assessment tools to sample cases from own teams and develop a plan for the same.
- Identify the different strategies needed for matching the aspirations of different people in their team.

Clear goals were set at the end of the programme. The programme was followed up with one-on-one sessions with the participants and, in the next three months, the company was able to lower attrition by a significant percentage.

While designing such interventions, we realized that the energies of trainers and organizations who commission training could be far better utilized, if there was a process to enable accurate determination of training needs that mapped completely with the business goals and strategies. In the following pages, we present a conceptual framework and tools for accurate DNA of an organization.

UNFOLDING THE ORGANIZATION DNA

Supposing is good, but finding out is better.
Mark Twain in Eruption

We propose a fresh approach to development needs analysis, taking the top down route for determining individual and team training requirements. This approach moves the development needs analysis process from the Training/ HR Manager's cabin to the strategic boardroom of an organization. The conceptual framework is given below:

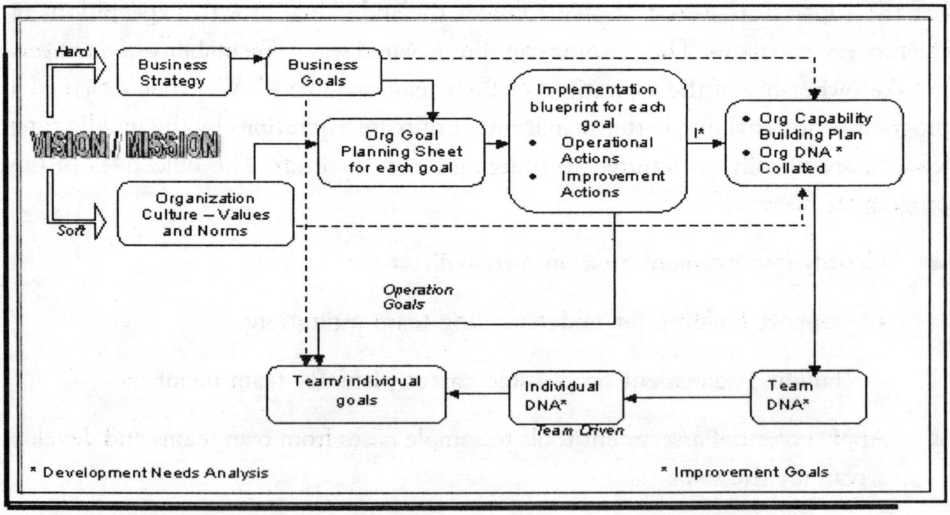

Figure 7 The Development Needs Analysis Process

The above model shows the process of determining development needs that are linked to the business goals of an organization. Let us understand the above model with the help of an example of an FMCG company, a leader in snack foods business.

The Vision/ Mission

The mission of this FMCG Company is " To achieve 100 million dollars revenue by the year 2005". This mission can be realized through two channels – hard and soft.

The Hard Channel

1. ***Business Strategy:*** Strategic concerns for achieving this mission were outlined. These were:
   - Right product portfolio backed by appropriate innovation template by organizing
     - R&D capability to meet innovation needs.
   - Get the right support systems in place to deliver them:
     - Expand distribution system – depth vs. width.
     - New plant by first quarter.
     - Fully utilize existing plant capacity on extruded line.
     - Managerial pipeline ahead of the growth curve.
   - Integrate logistics with operations.
   - New plant skill upgradation, introduce variable pay.
   - Drive for quality and compliance.
2. ***Business Goals:*** From the strategies flowed clear business goals, one of which has been chosen for our purpose of outlining the model further. This goal flowed from strategic concern of getting the right support systems._Production planning and supply chain process to become smooth and predictable, with no co-ordination problems resulting in no stockouts and minimum change of mix due to unavailability of material.

The Soft Channel

Organization Culture: The FMCG company in our example has defined the following value imperatives for its people:

i. Result orientation.

ii. Low response time.

iii. Pay for performance.
iv. Boundlessness vs silo thinking.
v. Ownership of team goals.
vi. Proactive vs reactive approach.
vii. Internal customer orientation.

Organization Goal Planning Sheet

The next step in the process provides a template for implementing the business goals in the form of the organization goal-planning sheet. We offer an adaptation of Phil Crosby's Process Model Sheet [5] as a tool for formulating the blueprint to achieve organization goals. A sample goal-planning sheet for the business goal chosen above for the FMCG company in our example is given below:

2. Key suppliers and inputs

1. Sales team
   - Sales planning forecast
   - Closing stock with distributor
   - Monthly sales plan
   - Plant finished goods position

5. Resources needed

a) Facilities & equipment	b) Structure, staffing, skilling	d) Budget highlights
• Increased storage space in the plant • Integrated planning software	• Role responsibility matrix • Systems orientation • Authentic speaking • Clear communication channels between people	• 4 Lacs for integrated planning software development

1. Goal

Production planning and supply chain process to become smooth and predictable

4. Processes & systems impacted

1. Material Requirement Planning system
2. MIS
3. Production planning system
4. Despatch planning
5. Sales forecasting
6. Review mechanisms, formal meetings

3. Key customers and outputs

1. Production team
   - Production plan
2. Sales team
   - MIS Information
3. Plant
   - Despatch plan
4. Vendors
   - Purchase orders

6. Planning for softer issues

a. Key decision makers	*b. Interaction between departments/ individuals*	*c. Problems faced/ envisaged*
• Director Operations • Director Finance • Manager Logistics • Manager Purchase • Category Planners • Production Planner	• Sales planner -Manager • Logistics/ Category planner-Purchase manager/ officer - • Commercial- Production planner - Despatch - Factory stores	• Ineffective communication flow • Focus on individual goals • Lack of respect for each others' role • Lack of trust in teams • Ambiguity in roles and responsibilities • Lack of goal and process ownership

Figure 8 Organization Goal Planning Sheet

Outputs from the Organizational Goal Planning Sheet (See Fig 8)

Implementation blueprint for "Production planning and supply chain process to become smooth and predictable" goal (from 4,5,6 c. in the organizational planning sheet - See Fig 8)			
Operational Actions • Establish systems for regular and effective review meetings • Review MIS Formats • Review storage space requirements	**By When** • Next fortnight • Next month • End of Q1	⇨	**Team and Individual Goals**
Improvement Actions • Role and competency mapping • Role and responsibility matrix • Prepare Process Maps • Develop architecture for new planning software	**By When** • Beginning of Q2 • Next fortnight • Next month • 2nd month of Q2	⇨	**Organization Capability Building Plan**
• Focus on team goals, win win attitude • Respect for each others' role • Trust in teams • Systems orientation • Authentic speaking • Operating new planning software • 360 degree feedback	**By When** } Ongoing • End of Q2 • Next month	⇨	**Organization Development Needs Analysis collated**

Figure 9 Implementation Blueprint for each goal

Blueprint of the intervention

After we completed the Development Needs Analysis using the process given above, we arrived at a blueprint of the intervention, in order to list down all the initiatives necessary to fulfill the needs. In this case, the proposed intervention looked like as follows:

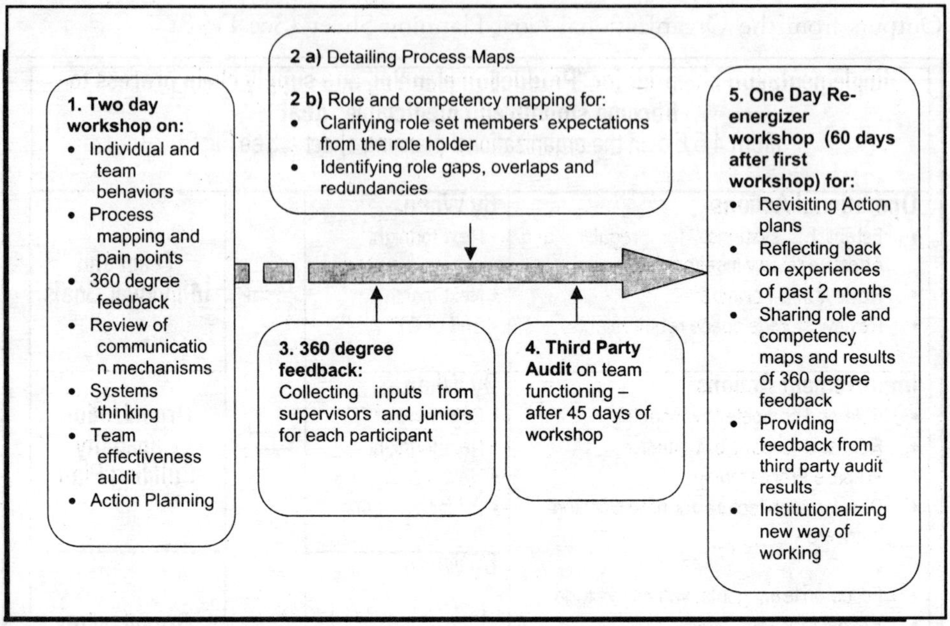

Figure 10 Blueprint of the intervention

As seen in the above blueprint, the complete intervention has a mix of systemic (role and competency profiling, process mapping), event based (360 degree feedback, third party audit) and training programme in order to achieve the business impact. Further, the objectives of the intervention were identified as:

At the end of the intervention, all participants will:

- Take ownership of common goal as greater than the personal goal.
- Internalize and practise effective team roles and behaviours.
- Develop role clarity and be better aligned with other team members.
- Arrive at solutions for the problem areas in the processes.
- Review the communication mechanisms within the purchases, supply chain and commercial teams.
- Set ground rules for team functioning .
- Practise systems thinking and develop internal customer orientation .

- Conduct an audit for team effectiveness and develop plans for improvement (individual and team based).

The intervention is still on but the impact of the first few steps are already showing. People are beginning to discuss their interpersonal and work related problems more openly. There is increased empathy for each others' problems. The supply chain team has started meeting regularly for reviews. Initial business results too are very encouraging and we are confident that the robust process we have employed will lead to the required strategic outcome of a smooth production and supply process.

Though we have illustrated the process for one goal, we could use it to come up with an comprehensive list of organization, team and individual DNA aligned to the business goals – displayed as the next few steps in the diagram.

Conclusion

Through this paper, we have tried to put down a new approach where the DNA is organically linked to business goals. We believe that the traditional process of obtaining training needs from the Performance Appraisal System has reached its expiry date. In Charles Handy's memorable words, its time we invented the second curve of the DNA process – only then can true learning organizations emerge. We owe it to Sumit and other participants of our training interventions. We believe that if Sumit's company develops its training programmes as an outcome of the Goal Planning Sheet, Sumit's cynicism will be transformed to positive anticipation at the beginning of a training programme, for he will know where and how he will apply the learnings. He will begin his walk with the end in mind.

So, instead of wasting effort in trying to climb the wall of training evaluation, a more fruitful enterprise will be putting the ladder against the wall of Development Needs Analysis to make this process more robust and scientific.

References

David Kolb, *"Experiential Learning Cycle"*

Donald L Kirkpatrick *"Techniques for Evaluating Training Programmes"*, in Evaluating Training Programmes, American Society for Training and Development, 1975

Jack J Phillips, "*Handbook of Training Evaluation and Measurement Methods*", Butterworth Heinemann, 1991,1997

Ferdinand Tesoro in "*Implementing Evaluation Systems and Processes*", American Society for Training and Development, 1998

Philip Crosby, "*Quality Education System - For the Individual*", Philip Crosby Associates Inc.

Acknowledgement

We thank the resource people in all the companies who participated in our research to provide us information about their training function.

CHAPTER

11

exploring career anchor—an unorthodox option for career management of indian IT professionals

PALLAB BANDYOPADHYAY*

* Pallab Bandyopadhyay is General Manager - Human Resources of Sasken Communication Technologies Ltd., a leading provider of telecommunications software services and solutions

Indian IT organizations are hardly making any serious attempt to initiate career management interventions for retention of IT professionals. Because of changing career needs, career management practises in the West have moved significantly from external perspective to an internal one. In internal framework of career the management, career is more subjective, pluralistic, owned and driven by individuals than organizations. In this framework, internal career needs play an equally important role in driving career satisfaction as that of external needs driven by organizational needs and constraints. There are not enough efforts made by HR managers in the IT industry to understand the internal career needs of IT professionals and use this data to plan effective career management plans. Career anchor, the occupational self- concept of individual can be an excellent tool to understand the unique career needs of IT professionals. Using this data, it is possible to design more innovative and pluralistic career management systems that can enhance the psychological contract between them and their organization and in

INTRODUCTION

It goes without saying that Indian IT organizations have realized that their business is knowledge dependent. Therefore, it has become imperative for them to retain their major repositories of knowledge - their employees. Being driven by technology, the Indian IT organizations are not only competing in a global market, where technology obsolescence is much faster, but also attrition rate of employees are much higher because of availability of wider career choices and employability of Indian IT professionals in the same global market. In today's scenario, the only true long term differentiator between two IT organizations is their ability to retain their knowledge workers; factors like technology edge, products etc cannot be the true differentiators since market forces will ensure parity on such parameters in the short term itself (Chandrasekharan, 1995). It is in this context, effective career management is emerging as a viable HR intervention to retain IT professionals. However, there has been a major concern both in industry circles as well as in the academia as to why Indian IT organizations are shying away from initiating this intervention. Inspite of the fact, that career management is known for addressing attrition issue, hardly any worthwhile effort has been initiated by HR managers to carry out systematic investigation to understand career needs of Indian IT professionals and use this knowledge to initiate career management programmes in organizations with a long-term perspective. As a matter of fact, career planning as an HR intervention in Indian IT organizations have always been neglected. According to Bandyopadhyay (1999), in Indian IT industry "**HR managers hardly attempted to make any value addition, by putting into place innovative HR interventions that strengthen individual-organization integration...Needless to say, why career development never figured in their priority list of HR interventions.**"

INDIAN IT INDUSTRY AND IT PROFESSIONALS

During last few years, the Indian IT industry has witnessed a very fast growth rate. It has contributed significantly to Indian economy by earning valuable foreign exchange through export of services and products.

Sachs and Bajpai (2000) identified Indian IT sector as a major contributor in moving India's place from 52 in 1999 to 49 in 2000 in the Global Competitiveness Report (GCR). According to them, the engine of growth of the booming Indian IT sector is the software industry that has grown at an average annual rate of 60% between 1992 and 1999. According to National Association of Software and Services Companies (NASSCOM) strategy report (2001), the number of IT professionals in India has grown from an insignificant base of 6800 in 1985-86 to 5,22,000 in March 2002. Their median age is 25 years and nearly 85% of them are male, 37% of them possess around 5 years of work experience. Their attrition rate generally hovers around 15%. Technical excellence, according to them was the reason why India was identified by 82% of US companies as their top destination for IT outsourcing, according to a World Bank survey. Realizing the strategic importance of IT for the country, the Indian government has set itself an ambitious target of making India a global IT power and a key contributor to the world IT industry by 2008.

Career Needs of Indian IT Professionals

Marketing research organization, Feedback (1999) conducted a study to devise appropriate strategies to attract and retain middle level IT professionals in India. The result of the study indicated that while pay, interesting work content and technology were high on the list of priorities for IT professionals, responsibility, recognition and growth prospects were also considered as equally important and appealing factors for their retention.

Lucent Technologies, Bangalore (1999) with the help from Gallup MBA conducted a pilot study. The objectives of this particular study were two fold:

1. To understand the mind of the Indian IT professionals; and
2. To collect 'leading indicators' to better align organizational strategy to individual needs.

The result of the study indicated that a) two out of three wanted to change the job in the next two years, b) one out of five wanted to settle down overseas for good and c) almost all felt that they were IT professionals first and employees next. Sahu and Gupta (1999) in their study conducted for Indian IT professionals looked at the empirical relationship between company image, pay satisfaction, nature of work, nature of peer team, comparison of peer team, inside career opportunities, expectation-reality match and turnover perceptions with intention to stay. It may be interesting to note that they found expectation –reality mismatch and outside career opportunities – were two major factors responsible for causing intention to quit.

Agarwal and Thite (2002) while looking at HR issues in Indian IT industry reported the phenomena of ***managing mixed motivation*** by most Indian IT professionals. They talked about how these professionals needed to manage expectations which seem to contradict between themselves from different quarters as part of their career. For example, while organizations want the IT professionals to work on projects as per customer requirements, their self expectation seems to look for opportunity to work on cutting - edge technology. While on one hand, the family expects monetary and tangible rewards, on the other hand the peers talk about opportunity to work on latest technology areas and overseas trip.

It is evident from the above data that the career needs of the Indian IT professionals are unique and need to be addressed through suitable career development interventions. In the backdrop of such realities, let us now examine how in this changing context, organizations can re-look at career management initiatives which can help in enhancing retention of Indian IT professionals.

The Perspective of External and Internal Career

According to Schein (1978), since both individuals and organizations exist in the context of the society; it is important to recognize that the societal culture through its value system would ultimately influence both the organizations and the people in terms of what is considered to be a good career. The concept has meaning to both an individual pursuing an occupation (the internal career) and the organization trying to set up a sensible growth and development path (external career) for the individual.

Thus, the core of internal career is the individual's self-concept within the context of organizations and occupations whereas the core of external career reflects ones own perception of organizational and occupational context itself. Derr and Laurent (1989) defined the internal career as *primary, subjective* and *owned* by the careerists and the external career as *objective* and reflecting a real world of *constraints* and *opportunities* in organizations and occupations. As aptly put by them, ***"....internal career is, What do I want from work, given my perceptions of who I am and what's possible?...........external career is, What's possible and realistic in my organization and occupation ,given my perceptions of the world of work?"***

However, historically, career management initiatives always focussed on external careers, often concentrating on devizing career management systems that culminated in a series of upward moves for individuals in the context of organizations with steadily increasing power, status, and compensation and so on. Though these processes were effective enough in the older days, they often failed to address changing career needs of knowledge workers. Way back in 1983, Yankelovich and Immerwahr talked about emergence of ***"Expressivism"*** among individuals in the context of twenty first century. As defined by them, it was nothing but internal and personal values - the need for fulfilling one's potential as an individual at work place. Similarly, Sellers (1994) defined modern day's workforce as generation X, which does not have interest in climbing corporate ladders or spending time in one type of job, instead they want to explore and do different kinds of job in order to learn about themselves and to express their individual values in the work settings.

Against the backdrop of these changes arrived the new definitions of career - "Protean Career" (Hall, 1976). The term protean is derived from the name of the

Greek God *Proteus,* who could change shape at will. Hall (1976) defined the protean career as a process, which the person, not the organization was managing and shaped more by the individual than by the organization. As put by Hall (1996) **"whereas in the past we decided to look more at the external career, the actual jobs or positions that a person holds over the course of the career, what seems to be more important now is the internal career, the persons perception and self constructions of career phenomena".** In this context of changing perspective of career, emerged a new contract between an employee and the employer, which is primarily psychological in nature. This term "psychological contract" (Levinson, 1962; Rousseau, 1995; Schein, 1978) is defined as a set of natural, often implicit expectations between the employer and the employee which functions like a contract in that if either party fails to meet the expectations, the impact could be serious, leading to demotivation, turnover, lack of advancement or termination.

Thus, it became evident that many of the traditional career management initiatives for addressing career issues became less valid today than they did twenty years ago. According to Arthur et.al. (1989) change in careers necessitated the change in conceptual perspectives necessary to understand them.

In today's context, IT organizations cannot achieve success without its employees achieving success. Therefore, the relationship between IT organizations and IT professionals also need to be looked from an increasingly symbiotic perspective. Needless to say, that the IT organizations need to think of initiating career management initiatives keeping in mind of this symbiotic relationship. An initiative that is based on the newer definition of employer – employee relationship. An initiative that moves away from the traditional perspective of objective and employer prescribed views of career to also understand and accept a subjective and individually perceived one.

The Concept of Career Anchor

Schein's (1975, 1978) development of the "Career Anchor" concept in assessing career orientation of individuals is a breakthrough in the direction of career research, in terms of shifting its focus from external to internal careers of individuals. According to Schein (1978), a person's "career anchor" is his or her occupational self-concept consisting of :

a) Self-perceived talents and abilities, (based on actual successes in a variety of work settings)

b) Self-perceived motives and needs (based on opportunities for self-tests and self–diagnosis in real situations and on feedback from others) and

c) Self-perceived attitudes and values (based on actual encounters between self and the norms and values of the employing organization and work setting).

The most important thing to note here is that the anchor is a **"stabilizing force"**- the values, motives and needs that an individual will not give up, if forced to make a choice. Starting his original research with Sloan school alumni in the mid 1970's, Schein's further research (1990, 1993) uncovered eight career anchors. With real life experience, feedback from peers and supervisors, and the emergence of their own perceived talents, people were found as belonging to the below mentioned eight career anchors.

Managerial: People who kept clawing right up the ladder with undiminizhed zeal. Their primary concern is to integrate the efforts of others, to be fully accountable for total results, and to tie different functions in an organization.

Technical/Functional: People who settled down happily to pay attention to the details of their craft. Their primary concern is to exercise their talents and skills in that particular area of expertize/specialization.

Security/Stability: People who discovered that promotions were rewarding largely because they meant, that the company prized them and wanted to keep them. Their primary concern is to stabilize their career so that they can relax and feel they have "made it".

Autonomy/Independence: People who found ways of carving out their own space in large organizations and are not ready to compromise on their freedom. Their primary concern is to free themselves from organizational rules and restrictions, in favour of developing a career in which you can decide when to work, on what to work, and how hard to work.

Entrepreneurial/Creativity: People who also ended up starting new ventures, products and services to meet their needs to be creative and to reap the benefits of their labours. Their primary concern is to create something new, involving the motivation to overcome obstacles, the willingness to run risks, and the desire for personal prominence in whatever is accomplished.

Service/Dedication: People who are dedicated to a particular cause, client group or ideology. Their primary concern is to achieve some value like helping others or making the world a better place to live etc.

Pure Challenge: People with primary concerns to solve unsolvable problems, to win out over tough opponents, and to surmount difficult obstacles .The process of winning is more central to them rather than a particular field or skill area.

Balance /Life- Style Integration: People with primary concerns to integrate family concerns, career concerns and concerns for self – development. They want to make all the major sectors of their life work together into an integrated whole.

Building on Schein's phenomenal work on career anchor, Derr (1986) came out with his concept of five diverse internal career orientations. While working with a group of U.S Navy officers, Derr developed this concept. Carrying out further research studies, he also validated the same in different fields and professional groups in the context of various types of organizational settings. These five types, which in many ways are actually similar to the career anchors described by Schein. These are described as follows:

Getting Ahead: These are people who are primarily interested to grow vertically and also much faster compared to their peers. They value competitiveness and by any measure of time, energy or emotional commitment, the job comes first to them.

Getting Secure: These are people who are motivated primarily by a sense of a job security and a life long organizational identity. Getting a secure career orientation defines success by the context of work rather than by the content or process of the work. They seek relatively stable environments where they can be more productive.

Getting Free: These are people who value autonomy most, which they are not ready to give up under any circumstances. In summary, these individuals run on freedom and are willing to do almost anything to get it.

Getting High: The objective here is getting challenging and exciting work, staying at the cutting edge. Derr (1986) described these people who "keenly want and need interesting and challenging opportunities to apply themselves; clear parameters or limits –time requirements, financial ceilings, rules to be observed, and within those limits support in the form of equipment, training, staff, application time and encouragement."

Getting Balanced: According to Derr (1986) "Career, self development and relationship with others – these are the three oranges that a getting balanced careerist is juggling all the time. If the juggling act is working perfectly, each orange has the same value and gets an equivalent amount of time. "This is a pattern in which individuals though include career goals and a high priority on work, keep the career remain in balance with self- development and relationship.

Looking At Career Anchor For Career Management Interventions

It is important for the HR practitioners to understand the career anchors of IT professionals, especially those which when fulfilled lead to strengthening the psychological contract. As a first step, it may therefore be logical, to explore career anchor as a viable means to understand these unique internal needs emanating from the differing career anchors. However, though it seems logical, the response from Indian IT organizations have been somewhat different at least in terms of making an effort to retain IT professionals by addressing their internal career needs.

According to Schein (1996), the metaphor of 'anchor' signifies that stability will be achieved in one's career if he/she is in an organizational environment that provides an opportunity to realize the components of his/her career anchor. Organizations create conducive environment for its people through innovative career management practises. Hence, it would be logical to assume that suitable career management practises could be instrumental in meeting diverse internal career needs of the individual. For example, an IT professional having autonomy as career anchor may value a career opportunity to create autonomous work teams, whereas the one with technical career anchor might like the concept of technical ladder in the career pathing and growth in the context of organization: for the third, security, posting at his home-town could be the instrument for satisfying his/her needs.

CONCLUSION

In the current scenario, there is an urgent need to design innovative career management practises that fulfils the diverse internal career anchors of individuals. Especially in IT organizations, where professionals have much more choices, it becomes imperative that HR mangers play a significant role in ensuring that career management practises are designed to cater to pluralistic career orientations of individuals. Dave Ulrich (1998) coined the term **"championing for employee's cause**"while propounding the new mandate for HR and included this as one of the emerging roles of HR for future successes. His statement – **"the new HR should be employees' voice in management discussions, offer employees opportunities for personal and professional growth",** summarises the paradigm shift that is required for HR managers to address the internal career needs of IT professionals.

It is expected that the HR professionals in Indian IT industry (a) would have a more pragmatic and pluralistic view of internal career diversity among IT professionals and (b) accordingly design suitable strategic career plan, which may address the internal career needs of IT professionals and reduce the usually high voluntary turnover prevalent in the industry. In this changing scenario, Indian IT organizations must realize that the time has arrived here too, where the professionals are becoming more pluralistic, where individual need fulfilment is becoming as important as the external ones imposed by demands, possibilities, and limitations of the organizations. Success in this industry will, therefore, depend upon the extent to which organizations adopt creative and unorthodox career management practises which takes into account both internal and external career perspective that can satisfy internal career needs of IT professionals and strengthen the psychological contract between them and their organizations. This pluralistic framework of career recognizes that there are seemingly different ways of defining career success for an IT professional in the context of organization and consequently markedly different approaches to career management to retain them.

References

Agrawal, N.M and Thite, M (2002): Human Resource Issues, Challenges and Strategies in Indian Software Services Industry (In Press).

Arthur, M.B., Hall, D.T., & Lawrence, B.S. (Eds.). (1989): The Handbook of Career Theory. New York: Cambridge University Press.

Bandyopadhyay, P (1999): Career Development in Indian Software Industry – Need for a Changed Paradigm. HRD News Letter, 15,4, October -December, pp. 30 – 35.

Chandrasekharan, M (1995): Culture Building in Start-ups, The Economic Times, Bangalore, Tuesday, 7th November.

Derr, C.B. (1986): Managing the New Careerists. San Fransisco: Josey-Bass, pp 8.

Derr,C.B. and Laurent,A.(1989):The Internal and External Career. In M.B.Arthur,D.T.Hall and B.S.Lawrence (Eds.).Handbook of Career Theory, pp 454 - 471,New York: Cambridge University Press.

Feedback Marketing Services Pvt. Ltd (1999): Key drivers – Middle management Software Professionals. Personal Communication.

Hall,D.T.(1976):Careers in Organizations. Glenview, IL: Scott, Foresman.

Hall,D.T.(1996):Long Live the Career A Relational Approach. In D.T.Hall and associates(Eds.).The Career is Dead : Long Live the Career, pp 1 – 12.

Levinson, H. (1962): Men, Management and Mental Health. Cambridge, MA: Harvard University Press.

Lucent Technologies India Ltd and Gallup MBA(1999):The Software Mind Map. Personal Communication

National Association of Software and Services Companies (2001): The Software Industry in India: A Strategic Review, New Delhi, India.

Rousseau, D.M. (1995): Psychological Contracts in Organizations: Understanding Written and Unwritten Agreements, Thousand Oaks, Ca: Sage.

Sachs.J and Bajpai.N. (2001): Miles to Go. India Today, February 19, 2001 pp 98.

Sahu, A and Gupta, M (1999): An Empirical Analysis of Employee Turnover in a Software Organization. Indian Journal of Industrial Research, 35 (1), July, pp.55-73.

Schein,E.H. (1975): How Career Anchors hold Executives to Career Paths. Personnel, 52(3), pp11 - 24.

Schein,E.H. (1978): Career Dynamics. Reading, MA: Addison - Wesley.

Schein,E.H. (1990): Career Anchors,Trainer's Manual. San Diego: Pfeiffer,Inc.

Schein, E.H. (1993): Career Anchor: Discovering Your Real Values. Jossey- Bass/ Pfeiffer, California.

Schein,E.H. (1996): Career Anchors Revisited: Implications for Career Development in the 21st century. Academy of Management Executive, 10(4), pp 80 – 88.

Sellers,P.(1994):Don't Call Me a Slacker. Fortune,Dec12,pp181- 186.

Yankelovich,D.and Immerwahr,J.(1983):The Emergence of Expressivism will Revolutionize the Contract between Workers and Employers. Personnel Administrator,28,pp 34 – 41.

Ulrich,D. (1998): A New Mandate for Human Resources. Harvard Business Review, January - February, pp 124 – 134.

Pallab Bandyopadhyay is currently working as General Manger (HR) with Sasken Comminication Technologies , Bangalore and can be contacted at pallab@sasken.com.

CHAPTER

12

effect of self esteem & mental health on the decision making capacity of managers

A K PANDEY*

* Dr A K Pandey, is Principal of Maheshwari Public School (A prestigious Senior secondary CBSE Affiliated School), at Jaipur.

The success of any organization largely depends upon the effectiveness with which it is managed and administered by its executive. It is a common theory that success and failure depends on place as well as on time. Psychologists differ in their opinions with regard to the characteristics and qualities of the managers which make him effective and efficient in his functioning. There is no denying the fact that managers require certain skills, technical, human and conceptual to become successful managers. Society today wants all these qualities in a manager plus something more. It is expected from them to be able to inspire those who work under their direction to achieve the corporate goal. Decision- making, communication and planning are the major functions of the administrators. Out of these, decision-making has got more emphasis than others. Their interrelationship has been argued by noting that one outcome of planning is a decision action, and that decisions would be difficult if not impossible to implement without a communication system. A decision can be defined as a conscious choice made from among a well-defined set of often competing alternatives. Decision is subjective and varies with the situation. The self-esteem, a person's idea about herself or himself is the most important single factor affecting behaviour and is directly related to the mental health. The present paper explores the role of self-esteem and mental health on decision-making capacity of the managers. The sample consists of 40 managers (30 male and 10 female). The findings reveal a significant relationship and the effect of self-esteem and mental health on decision-making process.

Individual differences are the root cause of individual thinking. Two rarely persons think alike. There are persons who are much ahead of others in reflection as well as in action. The quality of going ahead of others,is in a sense, leadership. Leadership has a number of attributes and decision-making is one of the main function of leadership. A leader must be able to reason logically and make decisions. Decision is a moment in the process of policy formation. It is much less than policy but in nature it is not different from it.In the context of organizational functioning, administration and decision making are largely-inseparable. Decision making is considered to be the heart of administration. It is the process through which administrator's work to accomplish their tasks. The power of an administrator in the organization is defined in terms of decisions that he is allowed to make. It is an administrative process which has important implications for human relations in an organization. It may be considered a culminating activity or the final phase in rendering a choice among alternatives, plus all activities that occur prior to it . Administration by eception, implies that managers conditions of conflict and collaboration are the main concern of leadership.

The word "self-esteem" has come into common use to refer to the individual who is known to himself. Concept of self are more or less perceptions of self which the individual regards as part or characteristic of his being. An individual learns about himself not only from his own explorations but also through his own mirror represented by the actions of those with whom he interacts. Many psychologists believe that the self has two aspects- concepts and feelings, and therefore, distinguish between 'self-concept' and 'self-esteem'. Self-esteem is the total organization of perceptions an individual has of himself. It is now a universally accepted fact that an individual's self-esteem, the value or judgement he places on himself and his behaviour have a say on his decision-making capacity. A great deal of emphasis is now laid on the study of self-esteem of individuals for understanding and predicting many aspects of their decision making capacities. Self-esteem is also considered as one of the dominating factors influencing the cognitive behaviour of an individual . Success and other pleasurable events in life lead to enhancement of self-esteem while failure, frustration and such experiences tend to lower it.

Mental health is an ingredient of personality .The study of personality gives us some of the aspects of mental health. Personality, in a general sense, is defined as your effect upon other people and this is directly related to mental health. An emotionally stable, socially useful and individually satisfying person claims to have a sound mental health. Virtually, mental health symbolizes the quality of the person. It is related more to emotional balance as it includes behaviour and other components of the mental health. In administration, a person's emotional control is the main thing which counts. How well the individual adjusts to life depends partly on which emotions predominate and how he expresses his dominant emotions. One great difference between a person who is emotionally disturbed and who is well adjusted is that, in the former, the negative or unpleasant emotions are more frequent and intense while, in the latter the positive and pleasant emotions are dominant. Gestalt psychology believes that if a person's behaviour is to be determined, his mental health must be taken into account.

OBJECTIVES

The present study had the following major objectives:

1. To investigate the relationship between decision-making capacity and self-esteem.
2. To investigate the relationship between decision-making capacity and mental health.

HYPOTHESES

The following hypotheses were proposed to be tested qualitatively as well as quantitatively:

1. There exists a high correlation between decision-making and self-esteem.
2. There exists a high correlation between decision-making and mental health.
3. There is a significant difference between male and female managers who were rated high on the criterion of decision-making.
4. Self-esteem and mental health when combined together are a good predictor of decision-making.

METHOD

Sample

The sample consisted of 40 managers of different factories who are involved with day to day decision making process. Out of these there were 10 female managers. Care was taken that the selected samples must be from a factory where not less than 800 people are working.

Tools

In the study the following tools were used:

1. Decision-Making Capacity Inventory (DMCI) constructed and standardized by Pandey (1995). It measures the decision-making capacity of managers. The reliability coefficient of the test is .86 and the validity coefficient .93.

2. Self-Esteem Measurement Questionnaire (SEMQ) constructed and standardized by Pandey (1997). It measures the self-esteem of the managers. The reliability coefficient of the test is .79 and the validity coefficient 87.

3. Mental Health Inventory (MHI) constructed and standardized by Pandey (1998). It measures the mental health relationship of the manager. The reliability coefficient of the test is .87 and the validity .93.

Procedure

All the individuals in the sample were approached individually and were requested to complete DMCI, SEMQ and MHI. The responses on the tests were scored according to the directions given in the respective manuals. The raw scores were then transformed to standard scores (Z-scores) for interpretation of data .

Statistical Analysis

1. Product moment coefficients of correlation were computed to study the relationship between decision-making capacity, self-esteem measurement and mental health measurement.

2. Two-tailed t-test was carried out to show that sex-difference plays a significant role in decision-making capacity.

3. Step-wise multiple regression analysis was used to identify the best set of predictor variables for decision-making capacity quality needed in management.

RESULTS

The date analysis revealed high correlation between decision-making capacity and self-esteem and human relationship (Table-1).

Table 1 Inter-Correlation Among Variables Under Study

S.No.	Variables	I	II	III
1	Decision –making	1.00		
2	Self-esteem	.74	1.00	
3	Human relationship	.83	.79	1.00

Significant at .01 level (df = 38, p <.01)

Step-wise multiple regression coefficient was calculated by Doolittle Methods. R was found to be .63 which was significant at .01 level ($p < .01$). R= .63 means that the score of decision-making predicted from the multiple regression equation correlated with the score obtained in self-esteem and human relationship.

The significant t-value showed that sex-difference play a significant role in decision-making capacity (Table 2)

Table 2 Male and Female Managers on Decision-Making

Group Compared	Mean	S.D	Difference in mean	SED	df	t	Level of significance
Male	181.36	3.42					
			5.24	3.23	38	1.37	p<.01
Female	176.12	2.41					

Significant at .01 level (df = 38, p <.01)

DISCUSSION

The findings reveal that the decision-making ability of individuals is highly influenced by their self-esteem and mental health factor. Multiple R shows that the correlation between decision-making may be predicted from the variables like self-esteem and mental health factor. It has already been interpreted that the above mentioned variables formed a good predictor of decision-making. R= .63 means that when the most probable score in decision-making which each of the 40 individuals will receive has been predicted from the multiple regression equation, the correlation between the predicted and the earned scores of 40 individuals will be .63. Multiple R tells us the extent to which the criterion measures of decision-making is determined by the combined action of the predictors. For the present study multiple correlation coefficient indicates the extent to which performance in decision-making is related to self-esteem and mental health factors.

Moreover, R is significant (p<. 01). It indicated that the predictors' formula in the form of multiple regression equation is a better predictor of performance in decision-making.

In this study, it has been found that male managers have more ability of decision-making than female managers. These findings lead us to the conclusion that high and low scores on the self-esteem and mental health factors are the main criterion of decision-making.

CHAPTER

13

hr @ the heart of business

VAISHALI BATRA*

---

* Vaishali Batra, is Manager - HRD with Hero Honda Motors Ltd., Delhi.

"Machines do not give us mass production. It is achieved both by machines and men. And while we have gone a long way toward perfecting our mechanical operations, we have not successfully written into our equations whatever complex factor represent man, the human element."

—Ford, quoted in C.Littler & G.Salaman

In the Global Village that is emerging today, economic companies risk being economic losers. A world of shrinking political barriers will need more and more living companies. This is because, paradoxically, the horizons of individual businesses are growing while political horizons shrink. There is a great temptation for companies to move out of their regional or national niche into a wider and therefore more unfamiliar environment. Even those that resist the temptation run the risk that the outside world will invade their home turf.

Overtime, fewer and fewer companies will live and work in an environment over which they have much control. More and more companies will be growing potatoes in the Andes rather than in a glasshouse. With their habitat shrinking, economic companies might become an endangered species – pushed back into isolated niches and legally protected national parks.

CHANGING WORLD ORDER

The electrifying pace of change faced by corporations today has not been seen before. The change does not confine itself to economics, political impact, information management or labour market in isolation or exhaustively. Change appears to have taken charge of running the business organization. The power and capabilities available to the corporation is competitively positioned for it to be leveraged and built or seems to be disappearing before our eyes. The complex business realities of the coming future will demand the ability to quickly and globally offer products and services to customers whose demands are never ending. Internal process will have to keep pace with this service demand. The challenge posed by this business upheaval would expect that competitiveness of the future world does not boundary base with technology, information and human resource. There appears to be a far-reaching and rapid integration of the business process to make the service to the customer happen.

These realities have necessitated the need for an organization to continuously evolve and get into a dynamic learning mode. A good learning environment is one in which managers are supportive and non-blaming and one where there is trust among colleagues. Employees are less creative when they feel they are being judged, when they have to compete and when their contributions go unrecognized. The effectiveness, degree and quality of learning depend on the circumstances in which work and learning happen. Attention to these circumstances makes a big difference for the learner and the outcome of learning. People learn by reflecting on their own experience, by sharing and by listening to the experiences of others. To allow this to happen, the environment has to be appropriate. Values are possible in several forms but the core human values, although exist in our soul, need speaking. They could be respect, value and dignity for the individual, care in consonance with nature, trust, mutuality, openness and transparency, integrity, equality, work ethos, positive attitude and standing by people in good and bad times. And it is important that values get propagated through and reflected in all our programmes and initiatives.

Global Mega Trends

- Economic considerations transcending political considerations.
- The movement of worldwide free trade.
- The powerful drive of telecommunications.
- The relative abundance of natural resources.
- Competition for reduced taxes.
- The Asian consumer boom.
- The advancement of democracy and the spread of free enterprise.
- Inflation and interest containment.
- The triumph of individual.

OVERVIEW OF INDIA'S ECONOMY

There was a time when foreign CEOs wouldn't even consider doing business in India. Between meddlesome economic policies (including restrictions on foreign investment), low education levels and corruption, India just wasn't an appealing place to invest. As growing foreign investment suggests, this is no longer the case. To be sure, conducting business in India is still fraught with difficulties, but

India's economy and business environment have come a long way in the last decade.

The improvements began in 1991, when the Indian government initiated a set of economic reforms. The results were impressive; India's GDP grew by about 7% a year during the mid-1990s. Foreign companies, already well aware of the cost advantages of doing business in India, have rushed in to take part in India's IT industry. In fact, NASSCOM reports that more than a third of Fortune 500 companies have outsourced some of their software requirements to India. But, IT is by no means India's only success story. Mumbai-based commercial banks ICICI and Housing Development Finance Corporation (HDFC) are among India's best-managed companies. And several magazines, including Forbes Global and the Far Eastern Economic Review rated Hindustan Lever, Unilever's Mumbai-based subsidiary, as among the world's best consumer household products companies.

Difficulties remain in some areas; however, India's economic reforms have helped to attract unprecedented levels of foreign investment. According to the Indian Reserve Bank, Foreign Direct Investment (FDI) mushroomed from almost nothing prior to 1991 to $3.5 billion by 1998.

Foreign Investment in India

Year	(A) Direct Investment	(B) Portfolio Investment	Total (A+B)
1990-91	**97**	**6**	**103**
1991-92	129	4	133
1992-93	**315**	**244**	**559**
1993-94	**586**	**3567**	**4153**
1994-95	1314	3824	5138
1995-96	**2144**	**2748**	**4892**
1996-97	2821	3312	6133
1997-98	**3557**	**1828**	**5385**
1998-99	2462	-61	2401
1999-00	**2155**	**3026**	**5181**

Source: Reserve Bank of India

Despite its substantial gains, India is still a very poor country with a per capita GDP of just US$2,200 when calculated using purchasing power parity, making the average Indian poorer than the average Zimbabwean. However, talking in terms of averages, when examining one of the most populous countries, can be misleading. Consider this paradox: India has a strong middle class of approximately 250 million people, comparable to the entire population of the U.S. despite the aforementioned per capita GDP. In fact, recently the Economist produced a survey on the Economic Outlook of India and handled this complexity by examining 'two Indias'.

Nevertheless, social indicators paint a revealing picture. Much of India is without telephones, and electricity. According to the 2001 CIA World Fact book, literacy

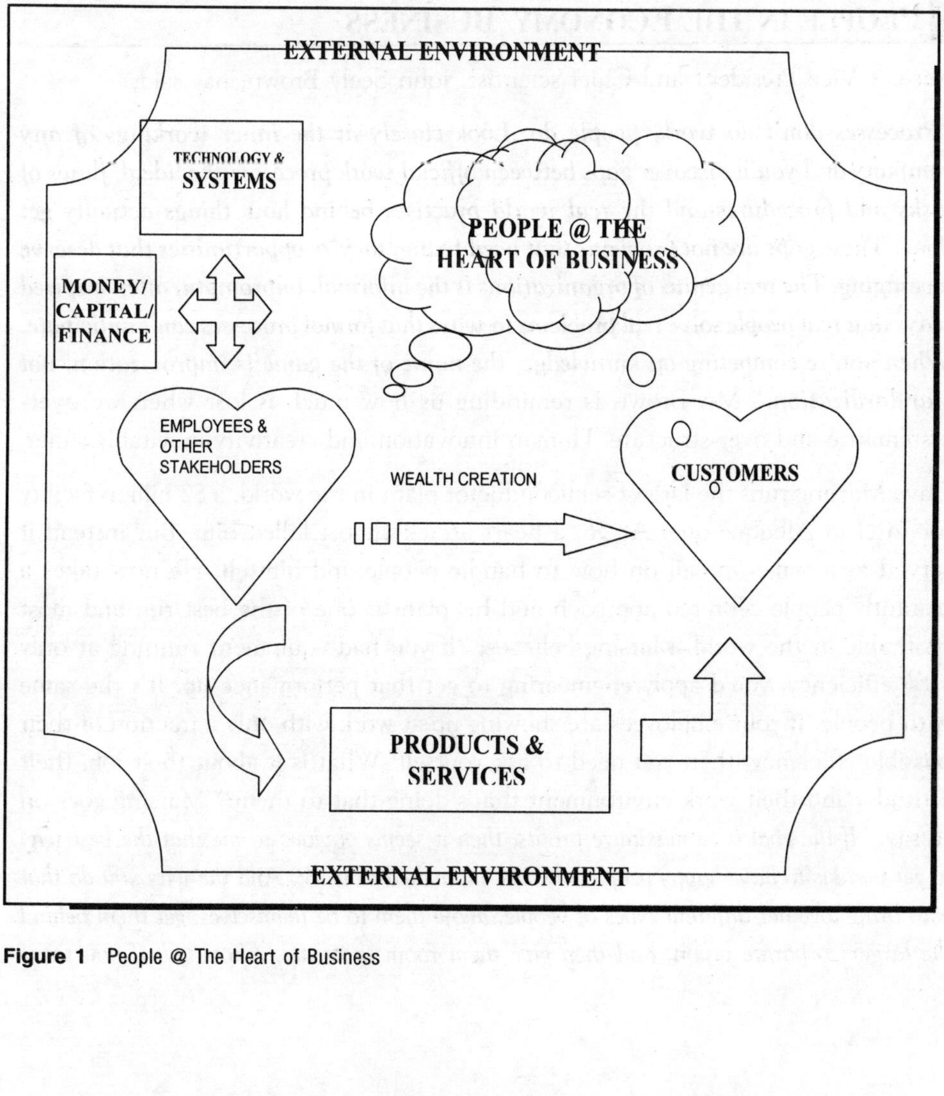

Figure 1 People @ The Heart of Business

in India stands at a miserable 52%.. And while growth in India's service sector has been strong, growth in heavy industry and manufacturing, which could provide badly needed unskilled jobs for India's poor, has not been as impressive. With these changes in our economy, coupled with the hypercompetitive global markets, the way business is conducted has also changed. Gone are the times when the people associated with the business were treated as commodities or another "factor of production". Now **people are @ the heart of the business. (Refer to the model below)**

PEOPLE IN THE ECONOMY/BUSINESS

Xerox's Vice President and Chief scientist, John Seely Brown, has said,

"Processes don't do work, people do. Look closely at the inner workings of any company and you'll discover gaps between official work processes-the 'ideal' flows of tasks and procedures-and the real world practises behind how things actually get done. These gaps are not problems that need fixing; they're opportunities that deserve leveraging. The real genius of organizations is the informal, impromptu, often inspired ways that real people solve real problems in ways that formal processes can't anticipate. When you're competing on knowledge, the name of the game is improvization, not standardization." Mr. Brown is reminding us how much is lost when we over-systematize and over-structure. Human innovation and creativity inevitably suffer.

Dave Marsing runs the largest semiconductor plant in the world, a $2 billion facility for Intel in Albuquerque. At 36, a heart attack almost killed him. But instead it served as a wake-up call on how to handle people and himself. He now takes a blatantly people-centered approach and his plant is one of the best run and most profitable in the world. Marsing believes: "If you had equipment running at only 10% efficiency, you'd apply engineering to get that performance up. It's the same with people. If your employees are showing up at work with only a fraction of their possible efficiency, then you need to ask yourself: What is it about their job, their attitude, and their work environment that's doing that to them?" Marsing goes on to say: "*If the goal is to maximize profits, then it seems obvious to me that the best way to get there is to have happy people who are motivated to work. And the way you do that is to bring together different types of people, allow them to be themselves, get them behind the larger corporate vision, and then give them room to create. Above all, if you want breakthrough and innovation - and you definitely do in this business to survive - then you have to cultivate those aspects of each employee's personality where it will come out."*

"If the rate of change inside an organization is less than the rate of change outside, the end is in sight."

—John F.Welch, Jr.

HUMAN RESOURCES, AS A FUNCTION, MUST BE EFFECTIVE

Historically, many human resources functions have acquired whatever power they had by serving as enforcers (the "HR police" role). While arguably there may be some power that accrues to this role, it is not the type of power that the human resources function needs in order to be successful in today's business world. In today's world, the type of power that human resources professionals must have, is the power to influence key decisions, the right to "play at the table" because their input is considered critical, not because the CEO or President says they have to be there. In order to earn this right, successful human resources, professionals must know the business (internal and external); understand and be able to integrate key people and business, economic and people drivers; be experts in communicating and operating across organizational boundaries; influence key decisions; and design and manage change.

THE MANUFACTURING SCENARIO & HHML

When Henry Ford proudly looked at the assembly-line winding its way on the shop-floor like a noisy car-vomiting snake, little would he have imagined that, soon this snake is going to be one of the most endangered species of its kind. The economies in mass production and in huge inventories have been unceremoniously cast away today in this customer – pampering competitive market. Buzzwords like right-sizing, downsizing, rationalization, and golden hand-shake have been welcomed by businesses while referring to the sheer number of employees. Manufacturing strategies such as "flexible manufacturing systems", "computer integrated manufacturing", "enterprise-wide resource planning" are making the rounds of the shop floors today. If this is the present, what is the scenario going to be in the foreseeable future? The future most definitely is going to be full of challenges, and businesses are going to be guided by continuous change on an uncertain & unclear path.

"World was never certain, will never be certain, only this.. is certain".

How the organization responds to the tremendous demands made by the market would be the key? The whole organization structure would need to be more organic than ever before, to be able to survive and remain world-class. The stringent and ever increasing demands of the discerning customer would mean that organizations respond to the demands of the market before the competitor does. The structure would have to be lean enough to create synergy and dynamism for disseminating communication quickly across all levels. On the other hand, the organization would require highly competent individuals who take the process of innovation and knowledge-enhancement seriously.

Let us try and visualize as to how different the future organization will be from today's organization:

TODAY'S ORGANISATION	TOMORROW'S ORGANISATION
Optimum organization	Minimalist organization
Specialized departments	Work groups
Less designations	No designations
Onus on participation	Onus on entrepreneurship
Career-driven employee	Knowledge-career driven employee

With this in mind, we look at how the concept of human resources, as a function, comprising of human resource development, employee relations, personnel management and establishment etc., is changing today. The employers of today are no longer paternalistic where what they said was to be followed by the employees. As the customers have awakened, so has the employee come of age? The successful organizations of today that want to survive in the future have to and are realizing the real assets of the company. *Human Resources now is the growth engine of the company*, and this is the direction we are moving in.

Hero Honda respects the dignity of human beings at all levels. In the matter of employment, it believes in the concept of equality of caste, religion, creed, race, sex and nationality. Employee selection is merit-based and made on the basis of proven ability of the incumbent (s). It is our endeavor to provide equal opportunity to all and one in the matter of internal promotions. Only the right person for the right job, however, is promoted. We are conscious of the fact that the growth and progress of our employees and the Company is inter-dependent, hence the concept of all round development of its team members is of prime importance. That is why we encourage meaningful participation of our team members to achieve the organizational goals and objectives. We strive to create an atmosphere where team-spirit and mutual understanding grows, dignity of labor is honored and sense of initiative is promoted in the working milieu. We believe that the problems and difficulties emanating out of day-to-day working be solved satisfactorily. Therefore we establish and promote direct contact with team members and try to eliminate the problems from the grass root level.

We at Hero Honda encourage and promote sports and such other cultural activities, which are useful in building the moral values and national character of honesty, discipline and integrity amongst all of us.

HHML's Mandate:

- Be a world class manufacturer
- Be the market leader
- Happiest customer is the Hero Honda customer.
- Achieve excellence through teamwork.
- Create enduring relation with stakeholders.

The Objectives of HR are:

- Developing a performance-driven culture
- Fostering a continuous learning culture
- Building an environment of cost competitiveness
- Promoting a participative & teamwork culture
- Fostering a total quality & customer-focused culture
- Improve employee well being & satisfaction
- Building relationship with stakeholders

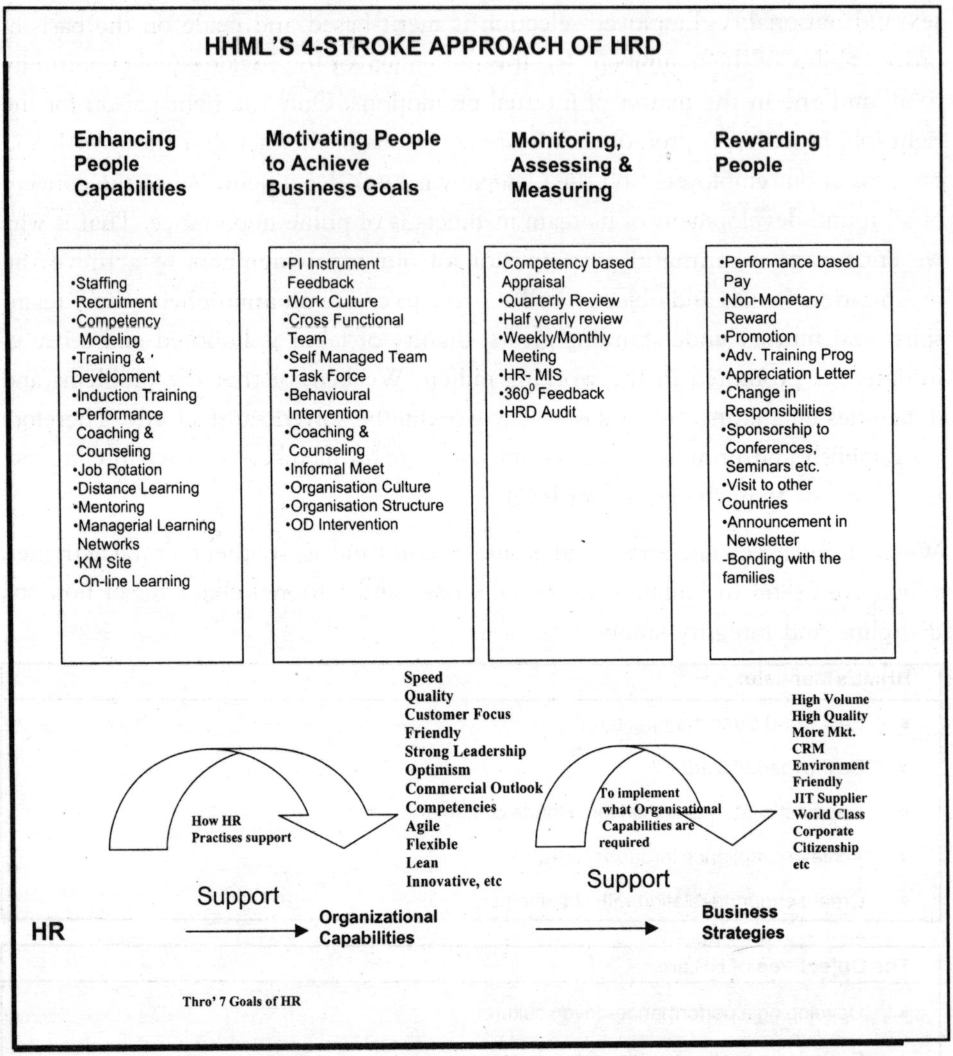

Figure 2 The 4 Strokes of HR @ HHML

To achieve real cultural change, the process must pervade the whole organization. We, at Hero Honda Motors Limited, do this through the various employee involvement programmes. Our commitment to our people is also reflected in our corporate objectives when we wish to offer joy to employees of manufacturing products of highest quality at a reasonable price. These serve as platforms for learning by doing and by sharing. In the organization building process, several factors continue to play a critical role in an on going organization. These include:

- Involvement and empowerment
- Productivity
- Quality
- Cost
- Technology
- Information
- Skills
- Systems
- Leadership

The various forums precisely aim at harnessing the potential of the people towards the above-mentioned factors. The practises and the programmes for generating employee participation are:

- Quality circles
- Suggestion schemes
- Cross-functional teams
- Open house
- Morning meetings

Extending the philosophy of **'We Care'** to the employees, we at **Hero Honda** have initiated a programme for the wives of our grass-root level of employees. It is a programme titled **'Grahini Vikas'** which aims at educating the wife about the positive influence she can bring in her husband's life.

The program in its first phase at Gurgaon has already covered 150 ladies in six batches. It is also reflective of the appreciation of factors outside one's work environment that affect an individual.

The three days training programme gives the participants a forum to express their views, share their experiences and learn from each other. Also, bonds get formed here, which are the foundations of relationships. The contents of the programme are specifically tailored to the profile of each batch. This is done keeping in mind the requirements of the particular group. Every day, for these three days for three hours each, these ladies are picked up from their homes, with kids, brought to the factory and later dropped back. There is a playroom developed for the kids with a ayah so that the mothers can concentrate on learning.

Day One sees a lady doctor from our Raman Munjal Hospital talk to the participants about family health, pregnancy, baby care, AIDS etc. The objective is to sensitize them towards their own health and also of their family.

The session on relationships on the second day demonstrates to her the positive role of a homemaker. It is more of experiential learning that happens at this stage. The variety of roles that a woman has to play at home proves to be the biggest challenge to her functioning at home. She is also given the basic inputs on budget so that she can help her husband plan for finances in the family. Safety-another critical issue at the domestic front is also touched upon to bring in awareness on its importance.

The third and the final day is a plant visit for the participants where they actually get to see how a motorcycle is produced. This brings in the realization of the value their spouse's work and efforts that go into it. Following this, is a presentation on the company, which educates them about the Hero Honda family. In the valediction function, certificates, photographs & a surprise gift is given to all the participants. The grand finale of the three days programme is the lunch for the couples.

The senior ladies of Hero Honda family, whose presence at the inauguration and the valediction is a source of our inspiration for all, have patronized 'Grahini Vikas'.

As our Chairman said in his address to the first batch, "You run this company from your homes and now you have to take it to greater heights," the message to all of them is clear.

The response to the programme has been positive both from the participants as well as their husbands. The ladies experience the 'Passion' of Hero Honda and the 'Joy' of being a part of the market leader.

All initiatives, practises and programmes are linked to the organizational excellence that is the overall way of working that balances stakeholders' concerns and increases the probability of long-term organizational success through operational, customer-related, financial and market-place excellence. This also takes us to the concept of "**living company**". A living company will have members, both people and institutions, who subscribe to a set of common values and who believe that the goals of the company allow them and help them to achieve their own individual goals. Both the company and its members have basic driving forces: they want to survive and, once the conditions for survival exist, they want to attain and expand their potential. The underlying contract between the company and its members (both individuals and other institutions) is that the members will be helped to reach their potential. It is understood that this, at the same time, is in the company's self-interest. The self-interest of the company stems from its understanding that the members' potential helps create the corporate potential.

The nature of this underlying contract creates trust, which results in levels of productivity that cannot be emulated by discipline and hierarchical control. Trust also allows space and tolerance, both inside the hierarchy and towards the outside world. These are basic conditions for the high levels of organizational learning that will, on occasion, be very necessary.

The organization is a community whose membership is variable, not only through individuals entering and leaving over time, but also by enlargement or reduction of the whole over time. This community has an identity – a persona-which continues to exist even when its composition changes.

Sometimes, members are forced out or converted into suppliers or contractors (a money relationship) – as when their value system is not harmonious with that of the company. This shift is healthy, because harmonized value systems are a basic requirement for corporate cohesion. Sometimes, reduction in membership takes place, because an inner group of members redefines 'us' and enlarges the definition of 'not us'. This may not be healthy, because of the shock to the trust levels of the remaining members.

The human members of a healthy company are mobile, both in the different jobs they perform during their careers and in the places where they perform those jobs. They network, they meet and they communicate across the whole organization.

There is mutual trust that people will act fairly and that the leaders are as honest as one could expect from human beings. People know their trade. Power is distributed; there are checks and balances in the power system and the present leaders understand that they are just one generation out of many still to come. Thus, this living company comprises of people, and ultimately serves people, hence the reality that people are @ the heart of the business.

CHAPTER

14

wired for change

A paper on e-HR presented to The National HRD Network, 8th National Conference "HR @ Heart of Business"

NITIN DHEER*

* Nitin Dheer, is Assistant Manager, Human Resources with Coca Cola India.

A misconception people and often, HR professionals have, is the fact that they believe, they have to adopt only the strategic role in the new economy.

– ***Dave Ulrich, HR Champions***

e – HR is not about solving the same problems, the same way, just without paper. Its...making better decisions, solving problems that could not be solved before and allowing decisions to be made much closer to the customer...

The following paper looks at the concept of e-HR and its application in the corporate world. The paper aims to clarify the concept of e-HR, its evolution and how it can add value to the HR function in an organization. It looks at two aspects, how e-HR is helping HR become a strategic partner to the business. Through its application, speed, reliability and transparency of the processes is getting enhanced. It also highlights some compelling examples of organizations which are benefiting through the use of technology enabled HR applications.

Finally, the paper seeks to provide a look at the future of the HR function in a technology enabled scenario. It talks about how in the future, the automation of all HR processes will lead to a complete eradication of the administrative side of HR and will lead to HR becoming a consulting function adding genuine value to the business as opposed to its current stage of being a support function.

E – HR The Future of Human Resources

Circa 1996, a fresh wide eyed batch of students join a premier business school in the country, with a dreamy vision of success, mega bucks, Learning and contribution to the corporate world. The young visionaries walk into their third class and the erudite professor goes round the class asking for career statements, one voice says I want to do HR, one says IR and Personnel Management, one says I want to be a HR consultant, one quaky voice pips in between the hackneyed career statements and says I want to be a CEO. The professor stops, seems a little taken aback, smile displaying years of stereotyping and condescension and says, well you are in the wrong class young man, we are developing human resource professionals out here. A HR professional's role is to 'partner a business' not 'lead' it. You can be a Head HR, but for becoming a CEO, well you will need to move out of HR."

The conditioning has begun!

The next few years are spent by professors, HR managers and business leaders reinforcing this organizational archetype of HR being a maintenance function with a large percentage of time spent in handling administrative tasks and a miniscule time spent in adding value to the organization. So by the time, the impressionable young visionary has traversed his initial three years of going through ' humility inducing experiences' the vision of being a business leader is just a collegial idealistic dream, which may be realized through serendipity, but as they all put it, "the businesses are not mature enough to accept this yet you can only change a system after becoming a part of it", and other sundry excuses and inadequacies for limiting that vision.

Through this paper we will look at two aspects, of how e-HR can aid the functioning of human resources in being a successful business partner and will explore the next dimension of taking HR along the lines of vision of our young B-School friend in making it a business leader.

The changing world we work and live in

"An economy is the way people use resources to fulfil their desires. The specific ways they do this, have changed several times through history and are shifting yet again - this time driven by three forces - Connectivity, Speed and the growth of Intangible Value. Because, we are so caught up in the whirlwind of this transition, we are experiencing it as a BLUR." Davis & Meyer - 1998

Take a look at the context of the current market and how it directly affects the role of HR. Right now, the previously well-defined boundaries, objectives, issues and opportunities within organizations have all become "blurred" – overlapping responsibilities, cross-market initiatives, performance imperatives reliant on new skills and experience – and all of these shifts in paradigm are happening at an ever-increasing pace.

- **Connectivity.** Everything is becoming electronically connected to everything else: products, people, companies, countries, everything.
- **Speed.** Every aspect of business and the connected organization operates and changes in real time.
- **Intangibles.** Every offer has both tangible and intangible economic value. The intangible is growing faster.

The most dramatic aspect of the "Blur" is this last point. The growth of intangible value and the drive to increase this value has not left HR unaffected. The most striking change in the new economy is the realization of the intangible economic value of human capital, and how that translates into fundamental business imperatives to attract, retain and develop that human capital.

A Business Case for Human Capital

Today's business environment is inducing organizations towards creating structures, processes and mechanisms that would enable them to treat their people as capital. The new model looks at organizing work around processes and not segmented tasks, creating flatter organizational structures that facilitate parallel instead of sequential information flows, making teams accountable and empower them for decision making, make organization boundaries permeable to bring teams closer to each other and also to customers and suppliers and encouraging skill enhancement and knowledge sharing.

The role of HR in this context becomes critical and also transcends the traditional boundaries which have limited it to a maintenance function. Each and every aspect of the above mentioned change in outlook is a function of quality of HR intervention in the organizational context. The interface and amalgamation of technology with HR, thus becomes an imperative in managing this transition as well as building measurable processes which augment the change.

HR in the virtual world

Responding to the increasing business imperatives above, HR has had to move with the times in order to cope. And in a world becoming more and more comfortable with access to real-time answers and solutions, HR has only one way to go – the transformation of systems, processes and outputs towards real-time delivery. HR professionals who have embraced the challenge have been able, in recent times, to adopt and (in some cases) innovate interactive HR transaction and delivery systems that meet flexible and highly fluid human capital needs. They have found the means to:

- Utilize technology as a strategic business tool.

- Organize a fluid company that embraces a culture and a desire to continually learn, innovate and advance.
- Challenge and outperform conventional recruiting.
- Improve and integrate hiring, appraisal, training & development, and succession planning.
- Investments in self-service at varying levels of complexity and value.
- Manage knowledge, learning and development, rewards administration and multi-directional organizational communication via personal portals.

What is e-HR?

The term e-HR is being used and abused. It now seems to cover anything from the use of sophisticated web-based HR systems with global access and automated administration down to simply having the term "human resources" on a company intranet. For the more forward-thinking HR professionals, systems enable employees and line managers to maintain basic personal data, review personal development plans, learn online, investigate and express interest in internal vacancies, confirm leave arrangements and a range of other administrative activities. These facilities are available from anywhere in the world with the appropriate security access in place. The results of taking this true e-HR approach include much-improved motivation levels, swifter processing and a big reduction in administration costs.

A survey conducted by consulting firm Watson Wyatt found that e-HR efforts built around savings and efficiency produced a measurable shareholder return, while those intended to enhance employee communication, which was a popular goal as e-HR, began to take hold in the late 1990s, actually correlated to a drop in shareholder value.

Steve McCormick, senior consultant at Watson Wyatt, says HR departments are now trying to leverage the savings provided by e-HR technology so that their function will be taken more seriously by CFOs and other C-level executives. "Historically, the perception of the HR department has not been very positive," he says. "But if technology can address the low-end administrative tasks, HR staff may be able to provide more valuable services." For example, he argues that while IT departments

Contd...

function as technology advocates, in most companies there's no "worker advocate" to focus on productivity, development and quality-of-life issues. If HR departments can tap low-cost technology to handle the paperwork, they can contribute in more substantive ways.

HR as a Strategic Business Partner

The effectiveness of HR as a strategic partner to businesses is a function of the relevance and the value it conveys to the organization. The efficiency and relevance of the HR processes is a function, of their speed, reliability, transparency and the ability to communicate their defined purpose. We will look at a scenario of an effective use of technology in the various HR processes to make them efficient, integrated and transparent, helping the human resources function effectively in partnering the business. We will draw from examples of their operation in various organizations.

The New Role of HR

Shown below is a model by Dave Ulrich (Human Resource Champions), which describes in terms of deliverables four key roles that HR professionals must fulfil to make their business partnership a reality.

Figure 1

The enabled HR organization

Lets look at the benefits that the e-HR option provides to an organization's HR processes.

Since we have addressed the issue of HR requiring to play a variety of roles and not merely restricting itself to the strategic aspects of its role. The question of **how to deliver HR services** in the future is a new question for most HR managers. But how companies answer this question may in fact **make or break** the effectiveness of their HR plans, policies and programmes in the future. And what makes the situation more critical is that businesses will need new HR programmes to compete in the marketplace and **new delivery methods** to reach the new worker.

We know from our research and demographic trends that the workers of the future will very likely be telecommuters; be self-directed in their careers; have a high need for challenging and satisfying work; be very impatient with inept management; and have little loyalty for their employer. An examination of the HR plans may be required—new plans for new people—along with new delivery methods to reach them.

There are a series of critically important issues that go to the heart of the role and value of the HR function itself embedded in the answer to the question since new delivery methods demand new technologies, vendor arrangements and new skills and competencies.

These issues include defining the amount and quality of support to the businesses, **capacity and speed** of a new HR programme introduction, cost of plan delivery and the level and form of service that will be supplied to the customers. It entails redefining what the HR professionals do in the future, when and how the company will use people to deliver services or use the Web or automated service centres, if they should invest more in their internal technology programme or if they should outsource their HR function entirely?

One thing is for sure...as HR starts looking at alternative delivery mechanisms for its transactional responsibilities, it will automatically result in freeing up more time to pursue the entire gamut of responsibilities that it is required to...

The diagram below provides an illustration of how the HR role would transform, as its involvement in transactional processes reduces as we move along the technology value chain.

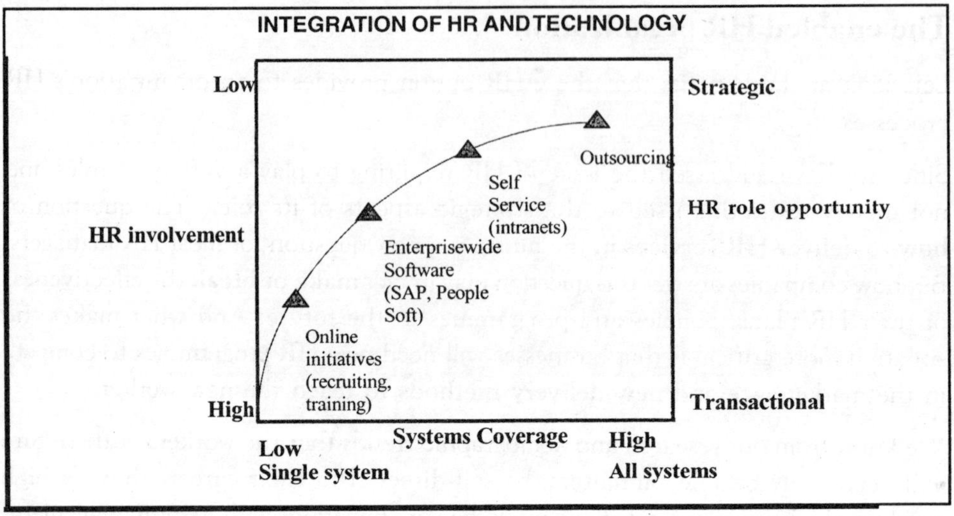

Figure 2

How do we leverage it…?

Technology for transaction automation…

. . such as payroll and automated benefits

> *For **Sodexho Marriott**, technology plays the dual role of **cutting administrative costs** through **systems automation** and providing a helping hand with more strategic tasks as well. "How to deploy recruiters, train employees, figure out who you want to keep and who you don't—we have a need for effective use of technology in each of those areas," says Harris. He also relies on technology to suck the costs out of those pesky yet necessary administrative chores. "You don't get a lot of credit for benefits administration," he explains. "People would rather have you spend money on the benefit than on its administration. My goal here is to pull money out of administration and put it into content and strategy. I don't care if we do it by outsourcing or by using technology tools ourselves," he says.*

Automation for convenience

. . through the use of Self service, HR kiosks, HR over the internet, real time systems

You'd think that employees would squawk at the prospect of more work appearing on their desks, but when it comes to HR self-service, most organizations who have tried it out would say that you are wrong. The model follows the ATM self-service strategy successfuly at banks and it's based on the theory that most people believe they can do the job best, be it getting cash or changing health benefits. Consequently, HR has pushed many chores out to individual workers, in the process cutting HR administrative costs. AT&T Corp., for example, has invested heavily in an HR intranet that employees use to get information on issues ranging from health insurance to pensions. Saving money was certainly an issue but so was "the speed at which change, and personal and professional business is conducted," says Lee Saviola, human resources director of benefits administration and technology integration at the Morristown, N.J., telecom company. People expect information more quickly today than in the past, Saviola says, and AT&T's Web site is populated with icons that represent what she calls life events, such as having a baby or retiring. Click on the retirement button, and up will pop a group of all the pertinent benefits.

Technology for internal customer service

Case: IBM understands these changing needs and delivers the only network computing application solution for Strategic Human Resources, Personnel Administration, Payroll and Benefits which addresses local and international needs: **HR Access.** The day-to-day burdens involved in administering benefit and other human resource (HR) programmes are enormous. These burdens are growing dramatically at a time when senior management is asking the HR function to move **beyond** administration and play a more strategic role in helping their organization's meet broad business objectives.

According to a recent survey by research firm Towers Perrin, the number of companies using HR self-service applications increased by more than 200 percent in 2000 versus the previous year.

Where are you on the e – journey?

Breadth: *Do you perform a number of different HR services — such as job postings and retirement planning — online?*

Access: *How many of your employees have access to a self-service kiosk or an intranet/ Internet connection to perform HR functions?*

Contd...

Strategic HR: *Is your company using web technology successfully enough to reduce administrative HR tasks and allow more time for strategic contributions such as employee recruiting and staffing?*

Integration: *Are you using the new web tools to link existing applications instead of relying on a single, monolithic system or a total out-sourced solution?*

Cost: *Have you made progress toward reducing your HR transaction costs by moving to online processing and self-service?*

How do we benefit from it...?

The benefits of a well-planned online HR service delivery mechanism turn up almost immediately in the form of increased productivity and reduced costs. Some companies recover the cost of building an intranet in less than three months and return on investment can be as high as 1,000 percent. With those kinds of numbers, it's not surprising that corporate intranets are proliferating as quickly as URLs in television commercials. Two out of three medium- and large-sized companies already have an intranet or are seriously considering one.

– 'Business–to–Employee Commerce, The hidden market', Mark Ranken with Theresa Mogavero

Enhanced ROI from e-HR

The technology enabled HR system has a positive return on investment, as it serves to replace recurring administrative costs through a system implementation. These costs relate to wage costs of the employees handling the administrative tasks, who can now be effectively re-deployed, overheads incurred on the administrative processes and sundry expenses on the same.

Enhanced customer value: The influx of technology in the HR processes, makes them fast and from the standpoint of customer service, this has the most significant impact. Also, with most of the administrative aspects of the processes being supported by a technology platform, the HR professionals are freed up to handle more value adding aspects of the same, enhancing customer value.

Saved hours...and money...with transactions and information presented online, HR employees end up saving at least 50 – 60% of their time allowing for a complete role transformation, as well as a reduction of organization expenditure on transactional HR, if we were to cost the total man-hours one puts in.

Saved paper...and printer toner...! By creating online forms, telephone lists, policy manuals, and the like, companies can save money on printing, packaging, warehousing, and shipping costs while offering better service to employees.

Intangible soft benefits typically focus on HR service improvement, but they are often more critical than hard-rupee savings.

Time compression... By successfully implementing an HR intranet site, tasks that once required layers of approvals and piles of paperwork are being automated, if not eliminated. Payroll, expense reimbursement, and recruiting via a company's intranet, also call for saving of hours and hours spent pouring over salary related excel spreadsheets, with calculators in one hand!

Increased accuracy... When employees are empowered to go online and update their own demographic or financial data, the data is more likely to be accurate which translates to a smoother process, and a lower return rate on inaccurate forms.

Improved feedback... Because of its ease of interaction, a website / intranet can help companies obtain valuable feedback from employees feedback that can help HR further improve service and support.

HR as a Business leader

The following section looks at the future of HR as a business leader, as a means to empower the organization in becoming an employer of choice for its employees.

The Human Resources Function of the Future – Vision 2010

Now we come to the last aspect–the aspect that our visionary on campus had grappled with. The desire to make HR a business leader. Lets look at the HR department of the future, which is enabled. In these times of fast change, HR has to change faster than the rest of the company, if it has to set an example and be a leader. HR cannot gain respect among executives if it is the weakest (slowest changing) link in the chain. The company's speed of change must be mirrored in HR products

So how do you do things faster, better and cheaper? Use technology in everything you do!

The HR Department of the Future

It is smaller and has a visible staff of only 3 people where there used to be nearly thirty. Besides the 3 HR people, there are no regular company employees wandering in and out asking questions and picking up forms. Even the name has changed…it is now called e-HR. Most employees (and HR people) work at home or are located around the world. There are no file cabinets, and not a paper "form" to be found. A paperless HR Department! All HR services are now done "remotely" and all transactions are now electronic, hence the title e-HR (Electronic HR).

e-Recruiting

All recruiting is now done on the web. Push technology allows us to send monthly e-mail newsletters and regular company job updates right to our target candidates. They no longer need to visit the web site. Students get an e-Letter (an e-mail newsletter) with exciting stuff to get them interested in the company early in their academic career. The managers can now take complete responsibility for all recruiting and hiring. Doing their own recruiting also puts them in better touch with the market and the needs of their new hires.

Resume robots and people "finder" programmes identify candidates effortlessly. On-line technical skills testing are now done remotely on the web before any candidate interview. These tools allow us to electronically compare these candidates with our "new hire success profile" which is automatically updated to ensure that every new hire "fits" our changing competency needs.

A web-based simulation "game" is used on all short-listed candidates. It electronically simulates the job they will have and assesses whether they have sufficient technical skills to continue on in the screening process. The next step is an in-depth web job simulator that allows potential candidates to be "final" screened to see if they can actually do the job tasks. The job simulator is so realistic (and it measures both current skills and the competencies for forecasting and assessing future problems), it beats any human interviews in validity and reliability.

e - Performance Management

Every employee has a custom designed on-line learning and growth plan to help them self-manage their career and to ensure they are continually challenged and are developing and growing as an employee. e-HR gets involved in coaching the managers only in the most difficult of the cases. In addition, a part of a manager's pay comes from attracting/retaining and developing their employees

e - Compensation

Centralized compensation was found to be too far removed from the customer to meet the changing needs of the business. Those old salary surveys that were only done once or twice a year were always out of date before they were printed. And the descriptions they used were often so generic that they didn't allow HR to use how to pay people as a competitive advantage over competitors.

The *"new" HR philosophy is to treat employees like "mature adults"*.

HR no longer needs a benefits department. Ninety percent of it is outsourced and the rest integrated into the new "Total Compensation" Department. Benefits are handled directly by third party providers. The employees give their information and benefits changes directly to the vendor firms on a self-service basis through the Internet. The extensive Intranet coupled with a direct click connection to the vendors makes answers to employee questions so easy to come by.

The compensation process owner's job is designing non-monetary incentives to help managers motivate their employees without spending money.

Managers do "all" HR

People decisions (hiring, pay, etc.) are the toughest ones. By being too control-oriented and by hoarding information, HR weakens management decision making. Weak decision making in the "people" areas seeps over into product decisions and that is really detrimental to the company. We let managers make million dollar decisions in plant and equipment but wouldn't let them give the receptionist a Rs 1,000 raise. So, now managers are provided with information and software tools that allow them to play out "what if" scenarios. Managers now have on-line job descriptions and performance appraisals. They have salary surveys that are updated daily by a network of headhunters. Now every manager has a software package that gives them equity guidelines and it also allows them to set their employees rewards without ever consulting HR. All salary changes are made by managers, without approval from compensation. Even when the salary varies beyond the preset equity guidelines on their computer, it is still automatically implemented (without approvals). The only "control" being that an e-mail copy is sent to HR. Managers are responsible and make all, people decisions. Technology allows managers to measure their own people performance on their manager's dashboard. HR coaches in the really tough cases but never decides or orders!

Proactive Control systems

A managerial quality identification survey on the Intranet periodically surveys employees on the quality of their management. If employees aren't challenged, recognized, get fair treatment or feel they don't have open communication, then their manager is given a review and action programme. And if it doesn't work they are cautioned and exited. Excellence in people management is a condition for continued employment.

HR monitors the people ROI. An "expert" software system monitors all people metrics on an employee "dashboard". These software tools act like "smoke detectors" (a kind of a thermometer) which warns HR in advance of potential people problems, so that HR can take preventative action.

Every employee is an HR person

As a result of strengthening managers' and employee's decision-making skills, the company makes great people decisions as well as great products. HR makes sure that the managers and employees "own" HR issues. We help with advice, when needed but HR doesn't really do any direct HR work any more! Technology and information allows high quality HR work to be shifted and owned by the people closest to the customers...managers and employees.

HR people

If managers do all compensation and hiring what is left for HR?

HR is now a Consulting Center. People come here for ideas on how to increase their employee's productivity. HR no longer just "runs" HR programmes and hold manager's hands, as HR people used to in the past. HR provides consulting advice, coaching and training in the use of the best "people tools and services" that lead to increased employee productivity. HR only helps in areas where we can actually increase productivity. For example, HR recommends electronic Intranet training because it has metrics to prove that it increases productivity and that has a positive ROI. HR educates managers as to what pay systems increase profit and productivity.

The best HR professionals (1/3) continue to work as strategic consultants and they love it. One third move out to become line managers (they have the highest success rate because of their people skills). The last third are happy to be gone. Most are" living in the past" as counselors or working in the community as social workers because they still really "like to work with people".

HR leaders can now easily become heroes in this organization. They are heroes because they aggressively use technology to enable others do more. The use of technology has given them a credibility they never had before. HR is no longer "begging" to be "at the table", ***people are now coming to HR and asking, "will you show us the way?"***

The only question that remains unanswered is "*who will organize the annual picnic*"?

A leader, not a partner and using technology to do all HR faster, better and cheaper – the HR department of the future.

